NATHANAEL WEST
The Ironic Prophet

NATHANAEL WEST

The Ironic Prophet

VICTOR
COMERCHERO

UNIVERSITY OF WASHINGTON PRESS
Seattle and London

Washington Paperback edition, 1967
Library of Congress Catalog Card Number 64-23342
Printed in the United States of America

to McCarthy

Contents

Acknowledgments

My thanks to all those authors cited throughout the pages of this study and especially to James F. Light for having supplied the biographical information required to support my inferences. I should like to thank Elaine Heise for inadvertently suggesting the title, and for suggesting to me just how emphatically archetypal West was as a writer.

Grateful acknowledgment is made to the publishers who have granted permission to quote from the following books:

The Hero With a Thousand Faces by Joseph Campbell. Copyright © 1949 by Bollingen Foundation, Inc., New York, N.Y.

From Ritual to Romance by Jessie L. Weston. Cambridge University Press.

The Complete Works of Nathanael West (containing *A Cool Million* and *The Dream Life of Balso Snell*). Farrar, Straus & Co., Inc.

The Day of the Locust by Nathanael West. Copyright 1939 by the Estate of Nathanael West. © 1962 by New Directions. Reprinted by permission of New Directions, Publishers.

Introduction to *The Day of the Locust*. Copyright 1950 by Richard B. Gehman. Reprinted by permission of New Directions, Publishers.

Miss Lonelyhearts by Nathanael West. Copyright 1933 by Nathanael West. © 1962 by New Directions. Reprinted by permission of New Directions, Publishers.

Finally, to all those critics of West whose works I have pored over, been intangibly influenced by, and now have forgotten, my sincerest thanks.

Foreword

AT FIRST GLANCE, Nathanael West has finally attained the heights of literary recognition. Both Alfred Kazin and Mark Schorer have recently listed a novel by West in their basic paperback libraries of modern American novels. However, a second glance at periodical bibliographies instead of trade newspapers forces one to re-examine his first impression. Moreover, while West is popular in college undergraduate courses, one still meets an occasional Ph.D. in American literature who has never heard of him. Most have never read West's novels.

Seven years after his rediscovery with the publication of *The Complete Works of Nathanael West* in 1957, it is difficult to understand the critical lag. With the exception of Stanley Edgar Hyman's excellent introduction to West as part of the University of Minnesota Pamphlets on American Writers, and a few fine articles among many poor ones, there has been little of value written on West, the one exception being James F. Light's biographical and critical study. My own more exclusively critical discussion represents an effort to extend the understanding of West's distinctive achievement and of the relevance of his work to our time.

I do not pretend to have written a thorough study of West; I am not sure I could, nor would I wish to do so. I have merely written a lengthy introduction. For the sake of completeness, I have included chapters on West's two minor novels, *The Dream Life of Balso Snell* and *A Cool Million.* Flawed works in themselves, they nevertheless have value in pointing out West's development as an artist. My approach has been critical in the main; I have, however, tried to point the way for other critics by suggesting West's influences as well as the dimension of his work.

If sometimes I have seemed to labor a point, ascribe it to my anxiety to convince. More often than not—and I am no exception —literary explorers of dark continents do not cut a neat swath through the jungle, they generally hack their way through. West's jungle was a more than usually difficult one, and one without much variety. If this study seems at times to be repetitive, it is because West is repetitive. Moreover, a study that is nearly as long as the entire output of the writer criticized, as this one is, will tend to suggest defects where they do not exist merely by revealing the artist's limitations—in West's case, his limited range.

I firmly believe that West, with all his shortcomings, is one of the dozen finest writers America has produced in this century, and that *Miss Lonelyhearts* and *The Day of the Locust* deserve a place among the best twentieth-century American novels. I have not written this study to assert that belief but merely to establish it. I hope that this study will act as a catalyst in rectifying West's critical imbalance, by convincing other critics that West is worthy of their serious, careful attention.

VICTOR COMERCHERO

California
Spring 1964

NATHANAEL WEST
The Ironic Prophet

I. Introduction

It already seems difficult, some mere half-dozen years after West's rediscovery, to recall that for many years he was nearly completely neglected. Some of this obscurity is understandable, for from the beginning his novels seem to have been beset by a series of almost comical calamities. *The Dream Life of Balso Snell* (1931) was privately printed (500 copies) by a small *avant-garde* firm; it was scarcely reviewed. *Miss Lonelyhearts* (1933) received mixed reviews—some of them scornful, even abusive—but the unfavorable reviews were far outnumbered by the favorable ones, and things began to look up. Liveright, the publisher, declared bankruptcy a few weeks later. *A Cool Million* was published in 1934 by Covici-Friede, a small firm, and almost immediately thereafter it went to the remainder tables and neglect. *The Day of the Locust,* published in 1939 by Random House, continued West's almost farcical publishing history, selling only 1,486 copies. A year later, three days before Christmas and one day after the death of F. Scott Fitzgerald, West, who was born October 17, 1903, was killed in an automobile accident with his young bride, Eileen McKenney of *My Sister Eileen* fame.

In themselves, West's publishing history and his neglect are only of passing interest. However, there is something in the riddle of shifting tastes that helps in understanding a writer's peculiar sensibility. Certainly, with respect to West, scarcely a critic has not been impressed by the fluctuations of his reputation. A few, in vigorous language, have taken up the implicit challenge and attempted to explain it. Alan Ross, it seems to me, has made the best attempt:

> West's slightness of reputation is not easy to understand, for *Miss Lonelyhearts* and *The Day of the Locust* rank almost with

> any novels that came out of America in the thirties—more condensed, penetrating and poetic than many, that with much larger scope and subsequent recognition, purported to give the lie to the American scene.
>
> Perhaps the ruthlessness of West's portrait, his making of the whole political and economic racket so undisguisedly repulsive and meaningless, was too near the bone for an American audience with a mass neurosis, and a guilty conscience.[1]

West has, perhaps unintentionally, explained it in his own fashion: "There is nothing to root for in my work. . . ."[2]

Prophets are hardly great rooters; and Jeremiah, with whom Tod Hackett (and, by implication, West) identified himself, was scarcely famed for his words of cheer and consolation. West's vision was a prophetic one, as his last novel, *The Day of the Locust,* indicates. The title (a prophetic symbol of catastrophe equivalent to the Day of Judgment) is justified by a final apocalyptic riot—the fitting culmination of West's vision.

West's pessimism and his preoccupation with decay, ugliness, perversion, and violence are conveyed with an Old Testament intensity which is disquieting. West, in his novels, suggests his personal involvement; and his two great novels, *Miss Lonelyhearts* and *The Day of the Locust,* are repressed, subtly dramatized Jeremiads.

Perhaps West was right; perhaps it was the unmitigated pessimism of his novels—a pessimism that made of every escape a cul-de-sac—which put off readers in the past. His novels dramatize the slow, lingering death of a civilization, either particularly, as in *Miss Lonelyhearts,* or generally, as in *The Day of the Locust.* The result is infinitely painful, for while premised on Old Testament morality, the novels recreate a world existing in a moral vacuum. West probably would have cringed at any association with a phrase so blatantly revelatory and potentially sentimental as "moral earnestness," but the association is unavoidable. For all his mocking laughter, West is seething with indignation, an indignation which, paradoxically, is grounded in compassion. The perplexing quality of West's two masterpieces results from his attempt to disguise his moral earnestness and his anguish by a brilliant comic imagination. Simply and perhaps extremely stated, he was an embarrassed moralist. He was also a frustrated one, for his nature and his world view made it impossible for him to "show the way"; he could only watch in fascinated horror at a wasteland before him that filled him with pity and rage.

Into this wasteland West threw his various stereotyped personalities representing peculiarly modern neurotic responses to the twentieth-century spiritual malaise. West must have shared some of these responses, for the stereotyped image he created was a personal one rooted in his observation of himself and the world around him. It was shaped with an eye for the sordid and grotesque and with an ear for the teeming vulgarities of our language. No other writer in America has done so much with ugliness and obscenity to create such fine works of art. West transcended his disturbing material by manipulating it psychologically. In doing so, he exploited psychoanalysis in a way which is almost without precedent. American literature has had earlier Freudians, but never before had a novelist of West's talent constructed psychological novels so devoid of psychological probing.

One could search West's novels with great care and never find a suggestion of introspective delicacy; one would not even find psychologically perceptive dialogue. That is not West's way. He is not interested in analyzing character; he is interested in crystallizing it by using Freudian images as symbols or objective correlatives of a psychological state. Intent on creating archetypal characters in an age of psychoanalysis, West probably felt that Freudian psychology was indispensable. But West is not interested in great subtlety; it is sufficient that the images convey the disorder.

The vague uneasiness we feel when reading West is often due to our subliminal perception of this Freudian dimension. It is not pleasant to be reminded as emphatically as West reminds us that our behavior is rooted in sexuality. It is particularly offensive when the proponent of such a view believes, not with Freud, in the potential beauty of sex and in the need to liberate its creative energy, but in the power and ugliness of sex, in sexuality as the opposite of spirituality.

Perhaps there is no need to probe deeply for reasons why West did not during his lifetime receive wider attention. His works induce too much guilt, and his ironies are such as to arouse horror and revulsion rather than pity. West is not content with Sophoclean ironies, such as Oedipus fleeing from his foster parents only to run into his real ones, or well-meaning menials bringing disaster upon their charge precisely because they are so well meaning. For West, such ironies contain enough horror, but they fail to suggest the squalor and moral ugliness of the twentieth century.

West's irony almost always induces a shudder of revulsion and of regret, for often we feel as if we have been taken in by an illusion which we are reluctant to give up. West is always disabusing us. For many, even those who fail to perceive the distasteful ironies, there is something seemingly unnecessary about the ruthlessness with which he proceeds to unmask illusion. His portraits are savage ones. He seems to strip his characters and, by implication, his readers of all dignity and respect. Yet, despite his seeming desire to remind us how unlovely his characters are, West is able to charge his ruthless prophetic vision with a dolorous compassion. Under a hard, mocking exterior, West was an extremely tender man.

Perhaps West's exploitation of sordid ironies was due to a reluctance to voice anything bordering on the sentimental, but more probably it was the inevitable culmination of his outrage and despair. The reason notwithstanding, it is West's ruthlessness, personal involvement, and violent intensity that create the ultimate tension which so exhausts the reader and so impresses him with West's stridency. There is no question that West is strident—prophets of doom usually are—and there is no question that he sets a rapid and hysterical pace, a pace which gives the reader little chance to catch his breath. The ruthlessness of the portrait and the rapid pace are inseparable; the country interlude in *Miss Lonelyhearts* is so moving precisely because it is the only resting place. (It may well be the only resting place in all of the novels.) Moreover, it is difficult to relax in the presence of the hideously disfigured, and there is something about West's characters that strikes us in this way. He had a peculiar feel for the sick "broken bastards" who inhabit the fringes of society; and in his novels these figures crawl out of the shadows into a bright light.

Dark as West's world view was,[3] it was probably the manner in which he translated that view into art that ultimately alienated his audience. West was both too European and too modern for an American audience bred on a national proletarian realism. Despite West's American idiom and topical setting, his influences were intensely European, as a casual glance reveals. In a list of major influences including Baudelaire and the French symbolists, the French surrealists, Kafka, Dostoevski, Joyce (and one suspects, Conrad), only T. S. Eliot can by any stretch of the imagination be considered American. Even Jung, Freud, mythology, mysticism, and the Bible had not been used in American literature quite the way West has used them.

Perhaps what puzzles us most about West is his distance from realism and naturalism. A keen observer, his effects are nightmarish rather than realistic. Always opposed to middle-class realism, West preferred a deeper level of reality, a preference probably derived from expressionists such as Kafka, and from surrealists such as Breton and Eluard, as well as their precursors Lautréamont and Apollinaire. Perhaps from them he learned that the most cruel but most efficient way to overcome conventionalized or dramatized feelings was to make fun of them. Probably from them he learned to shun the traditional forms of comedy and tragedy and to prefer a combination of the serious and the comic. To them he probably also owed his peculiar use of the grotesque. Always concerned with profound matters, West perhaps felt with them that "when Art is somewhat dominated by the grotesque . . . the spirit of modern man is more at ease in considering the serious, the tragic, the religious."[4] Equally derivative were certain aspects of his pessimism, such as a theatric sense of futility. Perhaps even his use of prophecy had its origin in surrealism, but more than likely, in tone and symbolism, he is most indebted in this respect to the Old Testament prophets. Finally, in his violent rejection of the human condition, he is surrealist, for "the idea of warfare against the purely human condition of man occupies the dark center and focus of surrealism."[5]

To Baudelaire, Rimbaud, and the symbolists, West probably owed his extraordinary inclination toward holocaust, toward a damned and sacrificed hero.[6] The influence of Baudelaire and the symbolists on West has already been noted by other critics,[7] but it can hardly be insisted upon too strenuously. The omnipresence of the scapegoat in West's fiction (there is one in every novel), while a temperamental predilection, probably is derived from Baudelaire, in whose work "we can read an apocalyptic resonance, a terrifying vision of man as sacrificial victim."[8] Moreover, West's created world, a blend of sordid realism and nightmarish fantasy, was probably influenced by Baudelaire's own created half-world.

Of equal if not perhaps of greater importance than Baudelaire or surrealism as an influence was T. S. Eliot, who himself was largely influenced by the symbolists. Like Eliot, West believed that art was not self-expression, and like Eliot, West's art deals with intensely personal experience, with internal conflicts and emotional dramas which are in some degree common to all men. Perhaps more important, from Eliot West derived some of his symbolism—particularly that of the wasteland; and his vision of the contemporary scene seems to have differed little from Eliot's, except for a suggested solution: West had none.

To discuss all of West's influences here would be impossible; some of them must be seen in context. West's reading offers us a clue to some of the writers who influenced him. These include Flaubert, Swift, Poe, Hemingway, Pound, and Sherwood Anderson. (Are Homer's hands inspired by Wing Biddlebaum's?)

It is impossible to explain West's public reception, past or present. It is tied up too intimately with literary currents and social forces. West was too modern for his time, and readers are only now beginning to catch up with him. Ultimately, it is irrelevant that his reputation has not been, and still is not, commensurate with the artistry of *Miss Lonelyhearts* and *The Day of the Locust*, two of the finest American novels of this century. We have the novels, and they are being read. That is what is relevant and what is important.

II. The Author Reveals Himself

FLAUBERT, for whom West had great admiration,[1] once declared, "*Madame Bovary, c'est moi,*" and "*Madame Bovary n'a rien de moi.*" Such an apparent contradiction is resolved when one realizes Flaubert's close identification with his heroine and, at the same time, his tendency to paint character impersonally as if it were pure object.

Such subjectively derived inspiration and such clinical objectivity of execution are even more characteristic of West. Even less farfetched than Flaubert's declarations would have been West's that Balso Snell, John Gilson, Beagle Darwin, Claude Estee, Tod Hackett, Shrike, and Miss Lonelyhearts "are all me and yet none of myself," for there is an element of self-revelation in West's writing so striking that it cannot be ignored. It is so basic an aspect of his artistic method that one cannot completely understand his work without taking note of it, and it is so frequent that it permeates his work. Two passages serve as illustration:

> When a baby, I affected all the customary poses: I "laughed the icy laughter of the soul," I uttered "universal sighs"; I sang in "silver-fire verse"; I smiled the "enigmatic smile"; I sought "azure and elliptical routes." In everything I was completely the mad poet. I was one of those "great despisers," whom Nietzche [*sic*] loved because "they are the great adorers; they are arrows of longing for the other shore." . . . You understand what I mean: like Rimbaud, I practiced having hallucinations.[2]

. . . . .

> Death is a very difficult thing for me to consider sincerely because I find certain precomposed judgments awaiting my method of consideration to render it absurd. No matter how I form my comment I attach to it the criticisms sentimental, satirical, formal.

> With these judgments there goes a series of literary associations which remove me still further from genuine feeling. The very act of recognizing Death, Love, Beauty—all the major subjects—has become, from literature and exercise, impossible. (*Balso Snell*, pp. 24-25)

It would be easy to dismiss all such remarks as applicable solely to the characters portrayed if their pertinency to West were not so striking, and if there were not a peculiar consistency in the sum total of such remarks. Moreover, one discovers that these analytic passages dotting the portraits of various characters are insufficient in their respective settings to create a single person. Individually, each of West's characters remains a caricature; cumulatively, they create an engrossing picture of a "type," of a "collective man" who has been created in West's own image.[3] What makes West's readers so painfully sensitive to the "Westian man" is an unconscious perception of the identification of author with character. The suggestive power of West's caricatures stems from their incomplete dissociation from real character. In lesser hands such psychoanalytic parallelism might be inartistic and offensive; more important, from a less sensitive intelligence incapable of experiencing and recreating complex, nuanced, and universal responses, such a method would fail to engage our emotions. That it succeeds in doing both is a tribute to West's talent and intelligence.

As one studies these analytic passages, one is struck by the nature of the self-revelation: West fails to use "real" incidents—that is to say, his self-revelation is rarely autobiographical. And when parallels exist between West and his characters, they are so muted as to be scarcely recognizable. Thus Homer's occupation as a hotel clerk vaguely recalls West's term at the Hotel Sutton; and Tod's position as a minor Hollywood designer or Claude Estee's as a successful screen writer is a slight switch on West, the minor Hollywood script writer. But even this highly transformed biographical self-revelation is extremely rare. The infrequency with which he used such experiences seems to be due not only to his antipathy toward pedestrian realism, to a surrealist belief that the subconscious offers a larger and more authentic clue to our being, but also to an innate shyness about dramatizing his objective existence. These factors largely shaped his art and made his creative world a half-world of impressions and mental states rather than one of substantial event. It is not strange, then, to find that West's characters reveal almost nothing about the author's life but a great deal about his psyche. Should this seem out of keeping with a shy temperament, one has only to note how muffled and ambiguous the revelation is to see West's complex attempt to disguise it. For all the exhibitionism of *Balso Snell*, West is basically secretive and retiring. Unlike Thomas Wolfe, he never pours forth his soul; and one never feels, with the possible exception, perhaps, in reading *Balso Snell*, that his self-revelation is cathartic: character development is neglected and analysis is so brief and pointed that the result is not nuanced character in all its multiplicity but personified attitudes and mental states simply and severely presented.

Intensely preoccupied by a few great problems, West created characters who not only crystallize such problems, but who, by a singular obsession, communicate his own intensity. Thus West uses his characters' grotesque obsessions—sometimes with something trivial, sometimes with something cosmic—to reveal his own. In this respect, one is again forced to use the Flaubertian analogy for purposes of clarification: to the extent that the characters are obsessed and, as a consequence, suffer, they are West; but because their obsession is literary—that is, exaggerated for dramatic purposes and so not exactly his own—they are nothing of him. In any event, it is clear that Westian man is essentially not a product of observation, but one of introspection. As a result of an enormous capacity for self-analysis, West was able to isolate the causes and manifestations of his mental states and to use them in his art. By dissecting his own personality, he was able to articulate psychological problems in sharp and concise terms. He did not, however, deal in generalities. His unique gift was his ability to create a semblance of character out of transfigured mental states. It is the ability to create personification, for in a significant sense West's characters are not created "in the round," with the human complexity which such a rounded portrait would entail; they are distillations. By means of this almost archetypal conception, West was able to recreate these transfigured mental states imagistically, without recourse to analysis. Had his world been more ordered, this ability would possibly have exhibited itself in allegory.

But allegory was impossible in West's disordered world. His characters do not arrange themselves into opposing camps of good and evil, or even of healthy and unhealthy—they are almost universally unhealthy; if there is any categorical division to be made in West's characters, it must be done in terms of their perceptions—those who are aware of "life" (the Westian personae: Balso Snell, Miss Lonelyhearts, Shrike, Tod Hackett, *et al.*) and those who are unaware (the Bettys, Fayes, and Lemuel Pitkins). Even this division is a trifle too neat, but nonetheless useful for purposes of illustration.

This disordered view of life is most evident in *Balso Snell* and *The Day of the Locust*, and these two works are the furthest from being allegory. That West's characters, once they become representative of an abstract "quality" or *idée fixe*, take on allegorical overtones is demonstrated by Miss Lonelyhearts.

West has described Miss Lonelyhearts as "the portrait of a priest of our time who has a religious experience. His case is classical . . ."[4] and, one might almost add, an allegory of modern man's frustrating search for meaning before the inexplicable existence of evil in this world. Despite West's apparently facetious presentation of Miss Lonelyhearts' quest, it would be an error to believe that he was anything but deadly serious in his statement of such a problem. James Light has suggested the prevalence of the quest motif in West's novels and has indicated his personal involvement in the theme:

> . . . if there is any constant pattern in the novels of West, it is the pilgrimage around which each novel centers. In each the hero is in search. . . .
>
> . . . more than likely . . . the reason West's novels are involved in the Quest is his rejection of a heritage, both familial and racial, that burdened West just as Joyce's heritage weighed on that great nay sayer. West's consciousness of his theme is evident from the beginning epigraph of *Balso* . . . and it is as a journey, dominated by a quest which ends in disillusionment, that West's novels should be read.[5]

Tormented by a sense of alienation, his near total, Dadaistic rejection in *Balso Snell* of all possible objects of identification—culture, religion, art, heritage and family—made it inevitable that he would remain a seeker, a "wrestler with doubts."[6] The questers who populate every one of West's novels are merely personae writhing under the same curse as their author. Their suffering troubles the reader not only because West analyzed and vividly recreated the intense neurotic anguish resulting from such a quest, but because he was able to transcend his personal involvement and render the quest in archetypal forms. In keeping with West's cul-de-sac pessimism, there is no Grail at the end of the quest. West had no answers and felt no need to do more than point to the seeker and to the nature of his suffering. "I believe there is a place for the fellow who yells fire and indicates where some of the smoke is coming from without actually dragging the hose to the spot. . . ."[7]

West here is merely justifying a role which his personal vision of life forced upon him. He could never "put out the fire" raised by the problems he treated; the paralyzing despair resulting from awareness and shattered dreams, as well as the presence of cosmic injustice are, among others, for him insoluble problems. Even when his problems become more sociological, as they do in his last novels, West offers no solutions. The reader of *The Day of the Locust*, has the terrifying feeling that he is watching the disintegration of a society; the ending with its apocalyptic overtones is part of the horrifying vision. The sense of helplessness he feels, resulting from West's ability to communicate the inevitability of the ending, may mirror West's own feeling. Perhaps some such "fatalism" may explain his willingness merely to point to the danger.

In a less sensitive individual, such a world view might become too insistent, might remain uncolored by subtle dependent attitudes; in West, however, it merely becomes a point of departure that led to the other attitudes and attributes which stamp his characters and his novels as uniquely his. In this respect, Robert M. Coates has pointed out that "West was fundamentally a pessimist . . . but he carried his pessimism a little further than did most other writers, to the point indeed where it colored his whole outlook on life."[8]

It is natural that West's pessimism should affect his entire world view when we recall that the pessimism is largely the result of discoveries made through introspection. Self-analysis, a method and seemingly a need in West, was also a source of pain: it made him extremely aware of his own responses, of his helplessness to control them, and of his near total helplessness before the "laws of life." His attitude toward introspection is clear: the consequences of the resultant awareness it brings are anguish or destruction; but those who are without the awareness are ignobly simple-minded:

> With the return of self-consciousness, he knew that only violence could make him supple. It was Betty, however, that he criticized. Her world was not the world and could never include the readers of his column. Her sureness was based on the power to limit experience arbitrarily. Moreover, his confusion was significant, while her order was not.[9]

West's desire and yet inability to solve the riddle of the world is mirrored here as clearly as is the importance and pain of self-consciousness. The partiality West reveals for his own state of mind does not offend; it is not only natural, but a direct consequence of his world view. In a meaningless world, nothing can have absolute meaning; however, a realization of such senseless disorder is more significant than a lack of it, and less dangerous, as West makes clear in *A Cool Million*. Neither alternative allows man to possess any great dignity, but somehow one feels that West gives whatever dignity is possible to those with awareness.

This theme of self-consciousness and its concomitant awareness rings like a bell throughout his work; and it is no accident that almost all his primary characters, with the deliberately striking offset exception of Lemuel Pitkin, are tortured by their introspective capacity. That it saves none of them and figuratively destroys them all is particularly revealing of West's own attitude.

There is little doubt that the destruction of his protagonists increases the power of West's novels; it nevertheless fails to render their fate tragic. More important, however, the characters do not gain one's sympathy—at least no more of it than they already possessed—by being destroyed. More often than not, their fate fails to engage one, and sometimes it strikes one as comic.

The characters in *Balso Snell* are too ridiculous ever to trouble West's audience, but even in *Miss Lonelyhearts* and *The Day of the Locust* reader identification diminishes as the novels progress.

Not only does the reader become less and less sympathetic to Miss Lonelyhearts' plight resulting from his increasing sensitivity to the letters, but his death itself in no way regains this lost sympathy. It does not increase his stature; if anything, it is so grotesquely comic that it almost disengages the reader. In like fashion, while Tod Hackett's consciously degrading fixation on Faye Greener both amuses and vaguely irritates, his breakdown at the end of the novel in no way engages the reader's emotions on the individual level; it merely adds to the general frenetic ending of the riot scene. Here again, one sees West's own ambivalent attitude toward introspection revealing itself. West did not like this "Hamletism" in himself; even though it was significant and necessary, it was too painful to be pleasant. There is an element of bitterness and of wistful regret, albeit carefully disguised, in the self-mockery of the following passage:

> An intelligent man finds it easy to laugh at himself, but his laughter is not sincere if it is thorough. If I could be Hamlet, or even a clown with a breaking heart 'neath his jester's motley, the role would be tolerable. But I always find it necessary to burlesque the mystery of feeling at its source; I must laugh at myself, and if the laugh is "bitter", I must laugh at the laugh. The ritual of feeling demands burlesque and, whether the burlesque is successful or not, a laugh. . . . (*Balso Snell,* p. 27)

Even without Jack Sanford's remark that West "hated . . . above all himself,"[10] such passages in West's novels would leave one with the uneasy feeling that West did not like himself. For him, such self-contempt is no crime; it is almost praise. It reflects the extreme idealist's usual dissatisfaction with himself for being less than perfect.

Seeing only the disparity between what he was and what he felt man should be, West tended to emphasize the ignoble aspects of his personality; he magnified their existence until minor flaws became great crimes. In a sense, he seems to have inherited that complex mixture of pride and metaphysical unworthiness that is a part of Jewish heritage. In West, this sense of unworthiness is magnified and generalized, for he was too realistic to fail to see that the bulk of mankind was considerably less perfect than himself. This realization did not, of course, make it easier for him to bear his own sexuality, artifice, self-deception, and a host of other real or imaginary faults. He had a certain prophetic Jewish idealism and intolerance that prevented him from extenuating man's frailty. He could have no sympathy for his faults and hence little for himself. In this respect, Beagle Darwin makes a comment which is especially revealing of West: "If I treated you savagely, I treated myself no gentler" (*Ibid.*, p. 47).

It is a deceptive remark when applied to West, for it glosses over his compassion. West's vision of man and of himself was a painful one, resulting in the seething indignation, in the savagely mocking laughter that marks his work. Yet he had a sense of sympathy for his characters—and for himself—which paradoxically seemed to forgive a great deal. James F. Light has attempted to explain the reader's ambivalent attitude toward West's characters by balancing West's sympathy toward his characters with his repulsion toward them:

> His [West's] attitude towards his characters shows sympathy, yet, at the same time, repulsion. Unlike his master Dostoevsky, West seldom seems able really to love the sordid people he depicts. Like Miss Lonelyhearts, West appears to be repelled by the primitive pathos he portrays, but unlike Miss Lonelyhearts, West seems unable to overcome the repugnance he feels for such sordid humanity. Sympathy, pity, he could give, but identification was beyond him. He could want to love, to lick lepers, but do it, he could not.[11]

Light's remark is revealing; but suggesting as it does a West closer to Miss Lonelyhearts than to Tod Hackett, closer to Christ than to the Old Testament prophets, it fails to seize upon West's anger and violent indignation. Nothing so well explains the ruthlessness of West's portrait, the savagery of his indictment, or the "ascetic, saintlike aversion to the flesh that comes through on nearly every page"[12] of his novels, as the contention that West felt compelled to assume a prophetic role. Yet, for all his prophetic idealism and intolerance, he lacked prophetic fervor or a prophet's sense of righteousness; he was too compassionate, too understanding, too humanitarian for either. It would not be stretching the matter unduly to apply the following comment, by Miss Lonelyhearts about himself, to West: "Humanity . . . I'm a humanity lover. All the broken bastards . . ." (*Miss Lonelyhearts*, p. 30).[13]

This tension between abstract intolerance and concrete love of humanity is not a new phenomenon in human nature, but it is an important one in West. It explains a reader's mixed feelings about West's characters and novels—feelings, paralleling those of the author, of compassion in spite of oneself and in spite of "objective reality." Had West not had the ability to feel sympathy for basically unsympathetic characters, the reader would not care about his characters. Because of West's vision, unlovely as the characters are, the reader still cares about them; he cares because he feels that West's indignation is not aroused by his characters but by the system, whether socioeconomic or metaphysical, which creates such characters. With the exception of the already mentioned degree of personal distaste West had for himself and therefore for one of his personae, West did not create unsympathetic grotesques because of a personal animus; he created them because they were emblematic of a cancer in the body politic and, at the same time, of the absurdity of existence. As a result, the reader's revulsion remains generalized. Even when dealing with sordid abnormalities, West generally charged the portrait with a compassion that more than counterbalanced the revulsion.

Norman Podhoretz has summed up West's ability to transcend both cynicism and sentimentality in order to arrive at a "strong-minded, intelligent compassion":

> It [the comedy of West] is also the animating principle of true sympathy, which is why West's "particular kind of joking" has so deep a kinship with the particular kind of compassion that is allied to intelligence and is therefore proof against the assaults of both sentimentality and cynicism.[14]

Any explanation for West's peculiar ambivalence is, of course, only partial, for it is difficult to isolate psychological reasons from esthetic ones. Certainly, as Light suggests, this tension between intolerance and love of humanity existed in West the man; but there is a hint that it was also a conscious intention. In an early essay on Euripides, West praised him for his fusion of feeling and satire,[15] and he probably considered such a fusion worthy of imitation. The following remark from *Balso Snell* is revealing: "What more filled with the essentials of great art?—pity and irony" (p. 51). Whatever the explanation, this fusion of compassion and indignation is the trademark of West's novels. All other factors notwithstanding, it is the natural consequence of the author's complex self-concept and projective method of creating character.

To say that West "created character" is to overstate the matter. West created character by donning masks. This tendency to speak through personae may not be applicable to his minor characters, who are different in kind rather than degree, but it is applicable to most of his male characters: the guide, John Gilson, Beagle Hamlet Darwin, and Balso Snell; Shrike and Miss Lonelyhearts; and Tod Hackett and Claude Estee in *The Day of the Locust.* Only such an explanation, it seems, can account sufficiently for the consistency of these characters and for the parallels their attitudes have with those of the author.

While it is not the object here to determine the exact degree of correspondence between West and his characters, there is much evidence to indicate that West's self-revelatory attitudes had a way of cropping up in disguised form. For example, West's hatred of "three-name women writers (Thyra Samter Winslow, Viola Brothers Shore)"[16] reached print in the form of a conversation in Delehanty's bar:

> One of them was complaining about the number of female writers.
> "And they've all got three names," he said. "Mary Roberts Wilcox, Ella Wheeler Catheter, Ford Mary Rinehart. . . ."
> Then some one started a train of stories by suggesting that what they all needed was a good rape. (*Miss Lonelyhearts,* p. 33)

The most striking example of West's true voice unintentionally emerging is found in his treatment of Jewish characters. In every one of West's novels, even in his finished masterpiece, *Miss Lonelyhearts,* there is a Jew to be found who is unsympathetic. In fact, it would be more accurate to say that West has created only offensive Jewish portraits. This fact could be dismissed as a not too uncommon manifestation of Jewish anti-Semitism if it were merely that; but it is not. Nor is it merely a defensive device, although it certainly seems to be that in part.[17] Rather, it seems to be the most startling example of West's need to treat personal problems in his work. What is so prominent about West's treatment of Jewish characters is his lack of detachment. His disguise is unsuccessful because it is strained.

Again one finds the peculiar tension in West's work between candor and secretiveness. In the revealing work *Balso Snell*, with the author apparently conscious of what he is doing, there is a secretive passage which reflects West's sensitivity to the entire Jewish question, to the complex play of identification and alienation often felt by Jews who have lost their faith. West's self-consciousness at being Jewish was too personal and too painful for him to reveal; he must disguise it. But as always, West's disguises are weakest when there is greatest involvement. In this passage, his involvement is so great that his objectivity fails him. The result is an overly violent reaction, which by its extremity is only that much more revealing. In this respect, the extreme Jewish caricatures West created are an example of his attempt at detachment. By creating obnoxious Jewish characters, he perhaps felt that he was proving his lack of involvement in the complex Jewish problem. It is interesting to see how his Jewish self-consciousness reveals itself through the mask when, early in *Balso Snell*, West introduces the problem:

> "What a hernia! What a hernia!"
>
> The guide began to sputter with rage and Balso tried to pacify him by making believe he had not meant the scenery. "Hernia," he said, rolling the word on his tongue. "What a pity childish associations cling to beautiful words such as hernia, making their use as names impossible. Hernia! What a beautiful name for a girl! Hernia Hornstein! Paresis Pearlberg! Paranoia Puntz! How much more pleasing to the ear [and what other sense should a name please?] than Faith Rabinowitz or Hope Hilkowitz."
>
> But Balso had only blundered again. "Sirrah!" the guide cried in an enormous voice, "I am a Jew! and whenever anything Jewish is mentioned, I find it necessary to say that I am a Jew. I'm a Jew! A Jew!"
>
> "Oh, you mistake me," Balso said, "I have nothing against the Jews. I admire the Jews; they are a thrifty race. Some of my best friends are Jews." But his protests availed him little until he thought to quote C. M. Doughty's epigram. "The semites," Balso said with great firmness, "are like to a man sitting in a cloaca to the eyes, and whose brows touch heaven." (*Balso Snell*, pp. 7-8)

That West himself probably could never have uttered the remark, "I am a Jew! and whenever anything Jewish is mentioned, I find it necessary to say that I am a Jew. I'm a Jew! A Jew!"

should not lead one to dismiss his identification with the guide. Certainly he was not that "type" of Jew, and he probably felt ashamed of and disgusted by such a person. However, this is beside the point, for writers are selective; they do not include in their works everything that they abhor. Nevertheless, by mocking an aspect of his existence, West had again dealt with a troublesome personal problem.

The subsequent remark by Balso Snell is arresting because Balso mouthes the usual non-Jewish line in an awkward situation. It is unnecessary to point out that West could never take such an approach; it is important, however, to make clear that Balso is the character with whom West is most closely identified throughout the novel. Furthermore, there is no reason to suppose that he has dropped his identification here. On the contrary, he seems to have increased it in order to show the impossibility of solving, and the ridiculousness of, the entire problem—of the guide's response, and of Balso's as well. He is merely using satiric irony and using two masks alternately in order to describe a real problem and to ridicule it out of existence by ironically pointing out the absurdity of both sides.

Such use of extreme masks is not unusual for West. He employs basically but two kinds of masks: the hopelessly unconscious and naïve, and the neurotically introspective. In both instances, the extremity of the posture is used to enhance the irony. West abruptly moves from the mask of naïveté to the mask of introspection—by far the more common one—in the person of John Gilson. Here West picks up a theme he is never to put down: self-consciousness and awareness. John Gilson's diary introduces the theme, and it never leaves the center of the journalistic stage thereafter. Two pages later, there comes the passage beginning "An intelligent man finds it easy to laugh at himself," a passage so tensely and mockingly self-conscious that one feels the author, in the manner of Rimbaud and the surrealists, must constantly have scrutinized himself as if he were another individual.

The consequences of the theme of self-consciousness seem so to have preoccupied West that he literally stops the movement of the novel to include "THE PAMPHLET," which is little more than a set of variations on the theme. He does not even bother to dramatize his self-revelation; his voice, for all its comic overtones, comes through the mask with disturbing clarity:

> While living with me, Saniette accepted my most desperate feats in somewhat the manner one watches the marvelous stunts of acrobats. Her casualness excited me so that I became more and more desperate in my performances. A tragedy with only one death is nothing in the theatre—why not two deaths? Why not a hundred? With some such idea as this in mind I exhibited my innermost organs: I wore my heart and genitals around my neck. At each exhibition I watched carefully to see how she received my performance—with a smile or with a tear. Though I exhibited myself as a clown, I wanted no mistakes to be made; I was a tragic clown.
>
> I have forgotten the time when I could look back at an affair with a woman and remember anything but a sequence of theatrical poses—poses that I assumed, no matter how aware I was of their ridiculousness, because they were amusing. All my acting has but one purpose, the attraction of the female.
>
> If it had been possible for me to attract by exhibiting a series of physical charms, my hatred would have been less. But I found it necessary to substitute strange conceits, wise and witty sayings, peculiar conduct. Art for the muscles, teeth, hair, of my rivals. (*Ibid.*, pp. 25-26)[18]

Though West has created an amusing passage, and one which introduces themes and characteristics recurrent in later works, his use of the mask here is rather pedestrian. One must turn to the Beagle Darwin passages of *Balso Snell* to see greater dexterity. Instead of using a mask to disguise a rather bare confession, as in "The Pamphlet," West employs two masks simultaneously, with one mask serving to analyze the other. Thus a close reading of the passage reveals that Janey Davenport, while holding the center of the stage, never actually speaks during the scene. Her words and thoughts are the figment of Beagle Darwin's imagination; it is he who, in the first letter, speaks for her and in the second, for himself. But West does not stop here. Characteristically, he pushes reality to an extreme that renders it absurd.

Introspection and imagined analysis of another person are not rare, but Beagle (whose middle name, significantly, is Hamlet), in an excess of self-conscious introspection, dons the mask of

Janey Davenport not only to analyze her but to have her analyze him. For all the apparent sophistication of Beagle's approach, his naïve egoism is unusually prominent. But West seems to be trying to do more than reveal the naïveté of exaggerated sophistication. By filtering knowledge three times—through West to Beagle, who imagines Janey analyzing him—West has made the very concept of "projective" analysis, of refracted perceptions, idiotic; and, at the same time, he has revealed how futile and egocentric awareness really is. It would take someone of West's talent and pessimism to give the irony that final unpleasant twist. To compound the joke, this bit of introspective delicacy takes place in a dream within a dream.

In its over-all context, the opening line of the letter is a fine example of West's ironic power: "Darling Janey: You persist in misunderstanding me. Please understand . . ." (*Ibid.*, p. 40). The substance of the self-revelatory mask, however, occurs a few paragraphs later:

> The ridiculous, the ridiculous, all day long he talks of nothing else but how ridiculous this, that, or the other thing is. And he means me. I am absurd. He is never satisfied with calling other people ridiculous, with him everything is ridiculous—himself, me. Of course I can laugh at Mother with him, or at the Hearth; but why must my own mother and home be ridiculous? I can laugh at Hobey, Joan, but I don't want to laugh at myself. I'm tired of laugh, laugh, laugh. I want to retain some portion of myself unlaughed at. There is something in me that I won't laugh at. I won't. I'll laugh at the outside world all he wants me to, but I won't, I don't want to laugh at my inner world. (*Ibid.*, p. 41)

One could continue to substantiate West's use of the mask to the point of tedium. Perhaps the most striking of numerous examples dealing with self-laughter is this glimpse of Harry Greener:

> He began to practice a variety of laughs, all of them theatrical, like a musician tuning up before a concert. He finally found the right one and let himself go. It was a victim's laugh.[19]

West's mark is on Harry as it is on all his characters. It is his voice that is vaguely heard, and it is this voice that stamps the characters as uniquely his. One cannot understand "Westian man" without hearing the voice and the peculiar barking laugh. One is not offended by West's repeated projection of his own image: his relatively small output, his irony, his ability to assume intriguing poses—in essence, his complexity and the incompleteness of his revelation preclude this.

If one attempts to explain the dramatic intensity of West's work, it must be done not only in terms of his style but in terms of the complex and ironic personality behind it. West seems to have had a peculiar schism in his make-up which left his emotions and intellect at war with each other. Thus, for all his emotional involvement, his savagery and bitterness, one finds an intellectual detachment which gave him his great ability to mock emotions at their source. As early as *Balso Snell*, and perhaps there most prevalently, one finds this peculiar schism.

The split had a skeptical base: in such a senseless world, how could anyone take anything seriously? As a result, in his life as in his work, West's "particular kind of joking"[20] was intended to show that the universe is always "rigged" against men and that their efforts against it are absurd. West's was the idealistic humanitarian's cynical laugh at himself and the world in an attempt to deny his own involvement in an agonizing perception. West mocked those aspects of existence that were most painful to him; as expected, the mockery became more violent as it became more personal. Thus, in *Balso Snell*, the most surrealistic of West's novels, and the product of his youth wherein one would expect the greatest emotional involvement, one finds him dissipating his intensity, as in the Saniette passages, through exuberant laughter.

The exaggerated expression characteristic of the entire novel is, to a large extent, defensive. West's adolescent identification with his characters was so strong, it was natural, West being the person he was, that it should reveal itself in such a manner. Moreover, as Fowlie has suggested, "There is a significant *rapprochement*, quite easy to make, between the adjectives *clowning* and *surrealist*."[21] But the pose of boisterous good humor was so unnatural to West that it could not be sustained.[22] He felt too deeply the problems he was dealing with, and this confining pose so prevented him from treating the problems seriously that he employed it only once again in *A Cool Million*.[23]

In *Miss Lonelyhearts* and *The Day of The Locust*, West assumed a pose more congenial to his basically serious nature. He was able to do so because he had moved away from surrealism (more so in the latter novel), because the works were the result of more mature conviction, and because these novels dealt with sociological as well as with generally insoluble psychological and philosophical problems—with the "human condition." The difficulties involved in a too boisterous expression of social criticism during the thirties are revealed in *A Cool Million*. Speculation as to the reasons for his growing "seriousness" aside, one clear impression emerges: West's examination of the human condition grew increasingly cool in his two major works. He was no longer suffering from the adolescent *Weltschmerz* he exhibited in *Balso Snell*; he no longer seemed to be the agonized young man who but recently discovered the presence of evil; he was, rather, in these works, a mature commentator who still remained involved in contemplation. In essence, he could treat the problems he dealt with seriously—within the limits of his proclivity to mockery—and with greater intensity, because of his increased detachment.[24] That he must continue to treat them is attested to by their recurrence.

Too realistic to shut his eyes, he was forced to express his particular world view; and whether accurate or not, his central message that life is empty and dreadful runs throughout all his works. The absoluteness of West's disillusionment paradoxically comforted him: prepared for the worst, he was hardly likely to be surprised. Defensive as his pessimism possibly was, it seems to have had as its wellspring his humanitarian idealism and his tender mentality.[25] If, because of the depth of his pessimism, West seems to reveal a surrealistic sense of futility and nihilism —*Balso Snell* is thoroughly destructive, and Shrike is a confirmed philosophic nihilist—one must never forget that West was a reflector of nihilism, not a disciple of it—another way of saying that, like the Dadaists and early surrealists, he was a forerunner of later writers of the absurd. Life was futile and senseless; hope was the greatest delusion; and, as with all delusions, it inevitably led to despair or destruction.

But West could not dress his pessimistic world view in serious garb. A straightforward, conscientiously held and delivered pessimism is too obviously a sign of total engagement; it too patently reveals the holder's emotional state. In his work, as in his life, he was embarrassed by his emotions. He did not, however, try to hide his pessimism—he felt it much too deeply to be able to do so—he merely tried to disguise his involvement in it. This camouflage he accomplished by "escaping" into irony.

To explain this ironic response as the natural consequence of a basically retiring temperament is to force the explanation: some of it undoubtedly results from symbolist and surrealist elements in his art. Yet, there is an element of secretiveness in West so considerable that it is difficult to resolve its existence alongside an admirable candor without turning to his low self-esteem. In these terms, his reticence not only becomes almost admirable, it also re-emphasizes his extreme sensitivity, a sensitivity so complex that the man would be more interesting than his work, were his work less the reflection of the man.

To classify this discussion of West's use of the mask as an example of the "intentional fallacy" appears to be too easy. The entire concept seems much more applicable to lyric poetry than to fiction. To insist on separating the author from his work in West's case is to insist on a fractional interpretation. One has great difficulty in understanding the subtle forces operating on West's apparently unsubtle characters unless one includes the author in any analysis of his work. In explaining the existence of one of the most powerful aspects of West's work—the suggestion of unspoken depths in his characters, or why his grotesques, while seeming to fail on the superficial level of reality, reveal a deeper one—it is necessary to turn to the subjective nature of his creation and to his ability to render such personal inspiration in enduring forms.

III. *A Study in Tension*

ENOUGH has been suggested to point out the influence of West's world view on his artistic method; in a sense, it resulted in his savagely defensive comic attitude. To a large extent, it is this characteristic of anguished humor, of blended pathos and comedy, that seems to be his trademark.

Perhaps an anecdote from his own experiences in Paris in 1924 will best reveal this characteristic as well as his paradoxical involvement in and yet detachment from the world:

> By the time I got to Paris, the business of being an artist had grown quite difficult. Aside from the fact that you were actually expected to create, the jury had changed. It no longer consisted of the tourists and the folks back home, but of your fellow artists. They were the ones who decided on the authenticity of your madness. Long hair and a rapt look wouldn't get you to first base. You had to have something new on the ball. Even dirt and sandals and calling Sargent a lousy painter was not enough. You had to be an original. Things were a good deal less innocent than they had been, and much more desperate.
>
> When I got to Montparnasse, all the obvious roles had been either dropped or were long played by experts. But I made a lucky hit. Instead of trying for strangeness I formalized and exaggerated the costume of a bond salesman. I wore carefully pressed Brooks Brothers clothing, sober but rich ties, and carried gloves and a tightly-rolled umbrella. My manners were elaborate and I professed great horror at the slightest breach of the conventional. It was a success. I was asked to all the parties.[1]

The problem is real, and yet it is put rather humorously; the detached self-mockery gives the comic quality. It is in this delicate balance between intense feeling and humorous expression that West achieves some of his greatest effects. Moreover, it is this balance that causes the state of tension one feels when reading his work. With only a slight tipping of the scales, the intensity of feeling comes through a little too strongly for laughter.

In *Miss Lonelyhearts*, the hero, who is writing a lovelorn column for the "New York *Post-Dispatch*," looks at one of his many letters:

> Dear Miss Lonelyhearts—
>
> I am sixteen years old now and I dont know what to do and would appreciate it if you could tell me what to do. When I was a little girl it was not so bad because I got used to the kids on the block makeing fun of me, but now I would like to have boy friends like the other girls and go out on Saturday nites, but no boy will take me because I was born without a nose—although I am a good dancer and have a nice shape and my father buys me pretty clothes.
>
> I sit and look at myself all day and cry. I have a big hole in the middle of my face that scares people even myself so I cant blame the boys for not wanting to take me out. My mother loves me, but she crys terrible when she looks at me.
>
> What did I do to deserve such a terrible bad fate? Even if I did do some bad things I didn't do any before I was a year old and I was born this way. I asked Papa and he says he doesnt know, but that maybe I did something in the other world before I was born or that maybe I was being punished for his sins. I dont believe that because he is a very nice man. Ought I commit suicide?
>
> Sincerely yours,
> Desperate (pp.3-4)

The artistry of humor is evident in the misspelled words, the poor grammar, the inarticulate groping for words, the naïve final question, and the absurdly ludricrous and yet characteristic pseudonym; and yet the reader does not laugh, or if he does, it is not with complete comfort. One is tempted to say that the problem is not funny. But such an explanation begs the issue. The problems in West's novels are never funny. It is only their expression that makes them comic. The answer seems to lie in the fact that the scales have been tipped and West's savage indignation has risen to the top.

A further illustration of the fragility of this balance can be seen in a passage from *The Dream Life of Balso Snell.* Coming across a diary in the bowels of the Trojan Horse, Balso begins to read:

> Jan. Ist—at home
>
> Whom do I fool by calling these pages a journal? Surely not you, Miss McGeeney. Alas! no-one. Nor is anyone fooled by the fact that I write in the first person. It is for this reason that I do not claim to have found these pages in a hollow tree. I am an honest man and feel badly about masks, cardboard noses, diaries, memoirs, letters from a Sabine farm, the theatre . . .
>
> However, I insist that I am an honest man. Reality troubles me as it must all honest men.
>
> . . . . .
>
> *Written while smelling the moistened forefinger of my left hand.* (pp. 13-14)

While West has pulled the rug from under his reader with the last sentence, the diversion has nothing to do with the problem dealt with. It continues to be no less a problem. However, the intensity is gone; West is laughing and so the reader laughs. Two such very obvious examples were chosen merely to dramatize the point; more often than not, the distinction is less obvious. It makes little difference that the latter selection is part of a parody of *Crime and Punishment.* Burlesque and exaggeration are recurrent patterns in West's art. The first selection is something of a burlesque as well, and yet one finds it difficult to laugh at it. It is not the burlesque that causes the reader's response as much as the nature of the emotive state West wants to arouse. He deliberately manipulates his art, charging it with intense anguish when he so desires and dissipating it when dissipation serves his purpose.

It is an oversimplification to say that language alone is the controlling factor. As in Stephen Crane and the early writing of Hemingway, there is a great disparity between the stated word and the response it evokes. Context and the author's emotional attitude seem to govern the reader's response. Such tonal nuance demands great control, and West is a controlled artist who understands the value of economy and understatement. He is rarely carried away with emotion.

By carefully maintaining a fine line between comedy and tragedy, West uses the comic both as relief and as preparation. By subtly alternating from one to the other, he heightens the reader's sensitivity to pathos and makes him almost helplessly receptive to slight shifts of tone. The result is a new and complex tension. The intensity grips the reader and the comedy detaches him so that he is paradoxically involved and yet, at the same time, detached. West does not allow the reader to become as involved as he is, for example, in an escapist work such as *The Odyssey*; nor does he allow him to become as detached as he is by some works of Kafka and Mann. The state of tension established between the reader as participant and the reader as spectator allows him to empathize with the characters while intellectualizing the events. In subtle ways, however, this emotional-intellectual complex increases the tension.

The ability to create subtle and complex tensions is one of West's finest achievements. A study of his style is, to a large extent, a study in tension. West's device, in creating a state of tension between the reader as participant and as spectator, allows for, and often demands, a comparison between reader and fictional character. The comparison is a spontaneous and unconscious one, but one that nevertheless tends to destroy reader empathy at the same time that it creates it. This paradox occurs because the reader is a participant and spectator on two levels: on the simple vicarious level, and on the experiential level. In essence, the reader not only observes the characters, he observes himself; not only does he participate empathetically in the characters' ordeal, he participates in a new emotion, much as if the work were a "real" stimulus to which he would respond. From the viewpoint of the masculine reader, this entire tension-producing process of observation and participation can easily be dramatized.

In *The Day of the Locust*, West early introduces this tension between the reader as participant and the reader as observer by juxtaposing possible but still grotesque incongruities in his description of Tod Hackett:

> His large, sprawling body, his slow blue eyes and sloppy grin made him seem completely without talent, almost doltish in fact.

> Yet, despite his appearance, he was really a very complicated young man with a whole set of personalities one inside the other like a nest of Chinese boxes. (p. 2)

The description is so sketchy that one fails to feel a human heartbeat in it. This failure alone would force the reader to keep his distance. Yet, West pushes him even farther away. The suggested stupidity of the character described in the first paragraph serves greatly to detach the reader; and yet the remark following intrigues him and so increases his involvement. It almost increases his desire to identify himself with the character. Taken together, the descriptions are both fascinating and repellent. One feels the same complex response even more intensely in watching Tod's infatuation with Faye Greener unveil itself.

The infatuation is a degrading one and consequently alienates the reader; at the same time, however, it is described with such brief but telling psychological verisimilitude that it arouses pity. Thus far, the relationship between reader and character is clear: the reader as spectator watches this spectacle of degradation with keen interest; as participant, he empathizes with the character's responses. As a result, the reader is fully capable of emotionally appreciating Tod's responses to Faye's dreamlike, sexually arousing storytelling.

> All these little stories, these little day-dreams of hers, were what gave such extraordinary color and mystery to her movements. She seemed always to be struggling in their soft grasp as though she were trying to run in a swamp. As he watched her, he felt sure that her lips must taste of blood and salt and that there must be a delicious weakness in her legs. His impulse wasn't to aid her to get free, but to throw her down in the soft, warm mud and keep her there.
>
> He expressed some of his desire by a grunt. If he only had the courage to throw himself on her. Nothing less violent than rape would do. The sensation he felt was like that he got when holding an egg in his hand. Not that she was fragile or even seemed fragile. It wasn't that. It was her completeness, her egglike self-sufficiency, that made him want to crush her. (p. 63)

The language, vivid and direct, captures one's feelings about such a woman so swiftly that for an instant there is no distance at all: the reader is almost pure participant.

West succeeds in destroying reader distance by several subtle techniques. Before beginning this passage, he allows Faye as an individual to fade into the background (her name is not mentioned in the three preceding pages) so that the reader is, in a sense, responding to an "idea," to an image of a certain "type" of woman. The effect produced is a strikingly direct response by the reader. The empathy is so total that for a moment he *is* Tod Hackett.

West destroys this near total empathy in the passages immediately following. With the sentence, "But he did nothing and she began to talk again," the close sense of identification is broken. West, in these following passages, not only disengages the reader, he arouses a feeling of revulsion in him. The revulsion, however, is touched with an unpleasant element of self-disgust. The reader as observer now perceives Tod in a new and degrading light. The fact that just prior to his new perception the reader has himself been the hero leaves him with a bad taste in his mouth. As a result, his emotional response to Tod's degradation is violently unsympathetic. The violence of the response is unnatural when studied within the context of the work but entirely natural when viewed within the context of reader ego involvement. The reader, in substance, has rapidly divorced himself from the experience and then, in a burst of self-defensive anger, rationalizes away his identification with the protagonist.

The subtle tension in West's work is complete. The very sense of identification the reader feels with the characters, because of their unpleasantness, results in an opposed movement of disengagement. The cycle is repeated over and over and to a large extent explains one's ambivalent response to the characters, that of mingled compassion and contempt. An examination of the manner in which West has succeeded in creating this tension explains in part why his psychological explanations and analytic descriptions are so powerful.

Such passages, generally short, concise units, are used to summarize a psychological state, the existence of which has already been suggested; or they are used to compress violently a response which has been building up for a great while. Not only do the suspense aroused and the culminating compression add to the intensity of the passages, but the language itself seems to clear up muddied responses by fixing them in a few hard sentences. Thus the emotions of frustration, passion, and hostility are crystallized in the remark, "nothing less violent than rape would do." By its forceful brevity, it results in arousing as well as reflecting such emotions. In this sense, the language has the aphoristic appeal of a propaganda pamphlet, but with a significant difference: West, though a master of rhetoric, never uses rhetoric for this purpose; he uses bald violence and understatement. A close analysis of the preceding passage shows how West manipulates language to gain maximum power.

The first paragraph is lyrical. Parallelism: "All these little stories, these little daydreams"; alliteration: "mystery to her movements," "she seemed always to be struggling in their soft grasp as though she were trying to run in a swamp"; and ripe, evocative language: "struggling in their soft grasp," "swamp," "lips must taste of blood and salt," "a delicious weakness in her legs," "soft, warm mud"—all are deliberately obvious. This is "decadent" writing. The sensuous language is too full, and it is intended to be so. It is the language of the "true romance" pulp magazines, only it is raised by its tricky tone and fine rhythm to a higher literary level. There are, however, enough erotic literary echoes to suggest, subconsciously, pornography and, therefore, to arouse the reader sexually even while amusing him. He may smile, but the language has nevertheless worked upon him its romantic power; he is caught up subtly in Tod's erotic reverie.

The second paragraph strikes with destructive staccato force, its power increased by contrast. The sentences seem clipped; they create a feeling of latent but crisp violence. West has set his reader up for a favorite combination: emotional relaxation (sometimes, tension) abruptly cut by clear and precise language which strikes the reader more forcefully because of the economy of the thoughts expressed. The contrast gives the second part of the passage a cruel, chiseled quality.

It would be erroneous to believe that West constantly resorts to soft language to create emotional relaxation or tension. More often than not, the language is neither soft nor extreme; it is, however, always "intellectually soft," emotionally arousing language. A glance at the following passage will show how the first paragraphs all prepare for the final one, a paragraph that fixes itself in the mind as if etched there in acid:

> Then some one started a train of stories by suggesting that what they [female writers] all needed was a good rape.
>
> "I knew a gal who was regular until she fell in with a group and went literary. She began writing for the little magazines about how much Beauty hurt her and ditched the boy friend who set up pins in a bowling alley. The guys on the block got sore and took her into the lots one night. About eight of them. They ganged her proper. . . ."
>
> "That's like the one they tell about another female writer. When this hard-boiled stuff first came in, she dropped the trick English accent and went in for scram and lam. She got to hanging around with a lot of mugs in a speak, gathering material for a novel. Well, the mugs didn't know they were picturesque and thought she was regular until the barkeep put them wise. They got her into the back room to teach her a new word and put the boots to her. They didn't let her out for three days. On the last day they sold tickets to niggers. . . ."
>
> Miss Lonelyhearts stopped listening. His friends would go on telling these stories until they were too drunk to talk. They were aware of their childishness, but did not know how else to revenge themselves. At college, and perhaps for a year afterwards, they had believed in literature, had believed in Beauty and in personal expression as an absolute end. When they lost this belief, they lost everything. Money and fame meant nothing to them. They were not worldly men. (*Miss Lonelyhearts*, pp. 33-35)

In this passage, one can see how intimately related to the emotional-intellectual contrast is the humorous-serious one. West constantly cuts open the comic surface with a neat razor-like incision that reveals a deadly serious bleeding ulcer. Like a surgeon, West sees the sordid significance and cancerous forces in operation, and knowing the case is hopeless at first glance, hurriedly sews up the patient. West never dallies in his dissection, he moves on rapidly—usually to more humorous problems. Invariably, however, the previous shadow seems to darken the humor.

The resulting tension is enormous; it is another instance of West's balance between intense feeling and humorous expression.

More than a random occurrence, it is a rhythm. The reader finds that his intellectual-emotional responses are determined by this rhythm.

His responses, of course, are not to a "representational" reality, but to an "underlying" one. West never deals with real events in the sense that the realist or naturalist does. His realism is thematic rather than factual, general rather than specific, mythopoeic rather than reportorial. An exponent of lean literature, West was impatient with the realistic and naturalistic novel and wrote: "For a hasty people, we are too patient with the Bucks, Dreisers, and Lewises."[2] Instead of documenting reality, he tried to enhance it. Thus his style is marked by distilled images devoid of minutiae and by short, active phrases heightened by an occasional colorful adjective:

> Around quitting time, Tod Hackett heard a great din on the road outside his office. The groan of leather mingled with the jangle of iron and over all beat the tattoo of a thousand hooves. He hurried to the window.
>
> An army of cavalry and foot was passing. It moved like a mob; its lines broken, as though fleeing from some terrible defeat. The dolmans of the hussars, the heavy shakos of the guards, Hanoverian light horse, with their flat leather caps and flowing red plumes, were all jumbled together in bobbing disorder. . . .
>
> While he watched, a little fat man, wearing a cork sun-helmet, polo shirt and knickers, darted around the corner of the building in pursuit of the army.
>
> "Stage Nine—you bastards—Stage Nine!" he screamed through a small megaphone.
>
> The cavalry put spurs to their horses and the infantry broke into a dogtrot. The little man in the cork hat ran after them, shaking his fist and cursing. (*The Day of the Locust*, p. 1)

A close reading of this brilliantly impressionistic passage shows the vividness of West's verbs and adjectives. For all its description, its effect is not descriptive: the sketch is too swiftly drawn. The result is a rapid scenic effect. By placing his characters in quick-moving, revealing situations, West was able to create scenes of such vigorous intensity as to be almost units in themselves. The technique, as the following two passages reveal, required economy; and more than anything else, it is this ability to seize upon striking yet bare images that explains the swiftness and brilliance of his writing.

> He entered the park at the North Gate and swallowed mouthfuls of the heavy shade that curtained its arch. He walked into the shadow of a lamp-post that lay on the path like a spear. It pierced him like a spear. (*Miss Lonelyhearts*, p.9)
>
> . . . . .
>
> Suddenly tired, he sat down on a bench. If he could only throw the stone. He searched the sky for a target. But the gray sky looked as if it had been rubbed with a soiled eraser. It held no angels, flaming crosses, olive bearing doves, wheels within wheels. Only a newspaper struggled in the air like a kite with a broken spine. (*Ibid.*, p. 11)

These two passages reveal the power of his stark images; a third, for all its apparent innocuousness, the extremity of his economy: it can hardly be carried further with success.

> He decided to go to Delehanty's for a drink. In the speakeasy, he discovered a group of his friends at the bar. They greeted him and went on talking. One of them was complaining about the number of female writers.
>
> "And they've all got three names. . . ." (*Ibid.*, p. 33)

Believing that accumulation of detail was not necessary to give a novel a sense of reality, West used it sparingly. Reality was to be met at a deeper expressionistic, psychological, or mythic level.

If the "spear" and "wheel within wheel" images (the last a traditional, quasi-religious emblem of order which occurs repeatedly in *Miss Lonelyhearts*) have not made it clear that West is a symbolist writer, the two passages quoted below should dispel any reservations one might have. West is a master of complex symbols, and *Miss Lonelyhearts* is his symbolic masterpiece:

> As a boy in his father's church, he had discovered that something stirred in him when he shouted the name of Christ, something secret and enormously powerful. He had played with this thing, but had never allowed it to come alive.
>
> He knew now what this thing was—hysteria, a snake whose scales are tiny mirrors in which the dead world takes on a semblance of life. And how dead the world is . . . a world of door-

knobs. He wondered if hysteria were really too steep a price to pay for bringing it to life.

For him, Christ was the most natural of excitements. Fixing his eyes on the image that hung on the wall, he began to chant: "Christ, Christ, Jesus Christ. Christ, Christ, Jesus Christ." But the moment the snake started to uncoil in his brain, he became frightened and closed his eyes. (*Ibid.*, pp. 20-21)

. . . . .

He fastened his eyes on the Christ that hung on the wall opposite his bed. As he stared at it, it became a bright fly, spinning with quick grace on a background of black velvet sprinkled with tiny nerve stars.

Everything else in the room was dead—chairs, table, pencils, clothes, books. He thought of this black world of things as a fish. And he was right, for it suddenly rose to the bright bait on the wall. It rose with a splash of music and he saw its shining silver belly.

Christ is life and light. (*Ibid.*, pp. 139-40)

The fishing imagery (and, by implication, sea imagery) which permeates the second passage is not accidental. West is recalling deliberately the Christ who was king of the "fishers of men." Less obvious and more suggestive is West's image of the snake, a nightmarish symbolic working out of Miss Lonelyhearts' repressed conflicts. The symbol is Freud's and, as to be expected, is phallic; the employment is West's. This yoking together of Christ with a phallic symbol, as we shall see later, creates an inevitable blurring of Miss Lonelyhearts' two conflicts: the religious and the sexual. West's symbolic brilliance, however, proceeds not from the abundance of symbols—although they are abundant, nor from their coherence—although they are generally clear and well integrated, but from their application. Perhaps so little has been made of West as a symbolist because his symbolism, like Kafka's, has not one application but several unrelated and seemingly contradictory ones. The obscurity occurs because West, attempting to suggest or evoke as many meanings as possible, seems to have taken pains to avoid overloading one symbolic interpretation at the expense of another. Thus West was careful to maintain the precarious tension between the mythic, religious, and psychoanalytic symbolisms in *Miss Lonelyhearts* in order that all three might remain operative.

This attempt to embrace many meanings[3] helps explain the disparate readings of *Miss Lonelyhearts.* The reader's interpretation will depend in large part upon his sensitivity to one set of symbols at the expense of the others. The sensitivity need not, of course, be a conscious one. It is necessary to realize that West, like Kafka, appeals to man's private instincts and deepest feelings, to that unconscious "nightmare world which is always just below the surface."[4] In such an appeal, as well as in his secretiveness, West reflects the influence both of the French symbolists such as Baudelaire and Mallarmé and of the French surrealists including Breton and Eluard. The influence of surrealism upon West was so considerable that despite his justifiable refusal to identify himself with the movement,[5] a knowledge of it is valuable in understanding his work.

Though undoubtedly influenced by Kafka, West's exploitation of the unconscious probably had its origins in surrealism; for the "discovery or conviction that we are more sincerely revealed in our dreams and in our purely instinctive actions than in our daily exterior habits of behavior (tea-drinking or cocktailing, etc.) is of course basic to surrealism."[6] Some of West's literary antirealism probably had its origin in such a conviction.

If the snake symbolism appeals to the unconscious, the fish imagery appeals to man's sense of the supernatural. The controversial nature of the passage with fish symbols and, indeed, of the ending of *Miss Lonelyhearts* has its roots in the failure of readers to realize that West in that novel exploited the "two qualities rigorously adhered to by surrealists—supernaturalism and irony."[7] Failure to perceive the irony is not entirely willful on the reader's part: much of it is due to West's peculiar sensibility and to his kinship to the surrealist movement. The elements of mystery and tragedy in West's work are "intimately related to the surrealist . . . hermeticism or obscurity or secretiveness in both the formalized aspect and the subject matter. [This is a quality which] perhaps best characterizes the intensity of the new art, and especially surrealist art."[8]

More obviously surrealistic is West's frequent use of dreams—*Balso Snell* is one prolonged dream which culminates in a nocturnal emission—together with decay, degeneracy and disintegration.[9] With surrealists, West often "used enormous incongruities to make his points,"[10] incongruities, however, which in his hands were both truly comic and savagely satiric. The comedy of incongruity is largely that of grotesque irony.

Grotesque elements, perhaps Kafkaesque and surrealist in origin, are a conspicuous part of West's method. Often, as in Tod's case, the grotesque consists of a combination of heterogeneous and incongruous details; but more often, it consists of distortion for artistic effect. Either way, the effect is disturbing. More than a stylistic device calculated to shock, the grotesque is a method of characterization: it gives his characters their unique, energetic individuality. If one is unable to conceive of West's characters in any other way, it is because they are described in no other way.

Perhaps even more important is West's ability to make grotesqueness atmospheric. West spends little time creating atmosphere, and yet it is always there. He creates it briefly, casually, as if in passing; but it is passed over so often that it seems never to leave the stage, an effect achieved by re-triggering a previous impression. A part thus serves to evoke a much greater grotesque whole.

Early in *The Day of the Locust,* West describes the people who inhabit Hollywood:

> As he walked along, he examined the evening crowd. A great many of the people wore sports clothes which were not really sports clothes. Their sweaters, knickers, slacks, blue flannel jackets with brass buttons were fancy dress. The fat lady in the yachting cap was going shopping, not boating; the man in the Norfolk jacket and Tyrolean hat was returning, not from a mountain, but an insurance office; and the girl in slacks and sneaks with a bandanna around her head had just left a switchboard, not a tennis court.
>
> Scattered among these masquerades were people of a different type. Their clothing was somber and badly cut, bought from mail-order houses. While the others moved rapidly, darting into stores and cocktail bars, they loitered on the corners or stood with their backs to the shop windows and stared at everyone who passed. When their stare was returned, their eyes filled with hatred. At this time Tod knew very little about them except that they had come to California to die. (p. 2)

The contrast between the two types has merely sharpened the

impression created by the latter group. West refers again and again, rhythmically, to these people who had "come to California to die," but always he uses such an image to suggest much more. The cumulative effect is overpowering. The images become generalized and emotionally charged. At the end of the novel, when he presents an unusually extended analytic sketch of the forces working upon these people, they have become so real that their brutal riot seems only to be the eruption of a natural, gradually mounting, long suppressed violence.

One could document this aspect of West's art at length. From Homer Simpson's hands and "deadness" to Miss Lonelyhearts, West's effect is grotesque. His brilliance, however, consists in his ability to intensify the portrait as the novel progresses. His novels, with the deliberate exception of *A Cool Million,* steadily build in intensity and end in a climax. Their movement is linear and rising, with no downturn and no denouement. When one considers the high atmospheric and descriptive level of tension with which the novels begin, this ascent is even more amazing. Because of this linear construction, West's choice of the short novel was a necessary one. Only in this way could he set the reader up for the emotional climax. It is the sense of gathering tension, achieved in part by numerous subtle rhythmic devices, that in large part contributes to the incredible power of his works.

It is not, however, these general considerations which make up West's unique style, but rather the fineness with which he polishes stylistic detail. The care with which West does so is revealed almost everywhere, but nowhere is it more evident than in the riot scene at the end of *The Day of the Locust.* It is perhaps the place one best can study his stylistic details and the unique effects he creates with them. The effect is achieved by the sharp, short sentences and by West's ability to select the right word in rapidly sketching the required material.

Thus, at the end of *The Day of the Locust,* West literally hurtles his reader into the riot scene by quickly and vividly capturing the ugly temper of the waiting crowd:

> A young man with a portable microphone was describing the scene. His rapid, hysterical voice was like that of a revivalist preacher whipping his congregation toward the ecstasy of fits. "What a crowd, folks! What a crowd! There must be ten thou-

> sand excited, screaming fans outside Kahn's Persian tonight. The police can't hold them. Here, listen to them roar."
>
> He held the microphone out and those near it obligingly roared for him.
>
> "Did you hear it? It's a bedlam, folks. A veritable bedlam! What excitement! Of all the premières I've attended, this is the most . . . the most . . . stupendous, folks. Can the police hold them? Can they? It doesn't look so, folks . . ."
>
> Another squad of police came charging up. The sergeant pleaded with the announcer to stand further back so the people couldn't hear him. His men threw themselves at the crowd. It allowed itself to be hustled and shoved out of habit and because it lacked an objective. It tolerated the police, just as a bull elephant does when he allows a small boy to drive him with a light stick.
>
> Tod could see very few people who looked tough, nor could he see any working men. The crowd was made up of the lower middle classes, every other person one of his torchbearers.
>
> Just as he came near the end of the lane, it closed in front of him with a heave, and he had to fight his way through. Someone knocked his hat off and when he stooped to pick it up, someone kicked him. He whirled around angrily and found himself surrounded by people who were laughing at him. He knew enough to laugh with them. (pp. 155-56)

In less than three hundred words, West deeply involves the reader in the scene. Then, in slightly more than a page of exposition, he sets the stage for the riot. He paves the way through action. This is a frequent characteristic of West's method: rapid preliminary action; a brief, colorful bit of exposition; and finally, the dramatic climax of the scene.

A brief analysis of the riot scene reveals the amount of compression involved in this method. First, the initial simile of the revivalist preacher, although it seems to stand alone, molds the reader's response to the announcer's speech. West's ear for dialogue is evident: the announcer's language is deliberately extreme, but not so much that it is not credible. Reality is preserved but made comic.

West then introduces a new relationship: that between the crowd and the police. When he begins to describe the crowd's response to the police, he is rather offhanded, as if the explanation is an afterthought: "It allowed itself to be hustled and shoved out of habit and because it lacked an objective." The passive voice is used to convey the mood of the crowd itself in a subtle and extremely suggestive form of understatement. Then, in a rather incongruous but appropriate simile, West reinforces the impression of passive power represented by the crowd: "It tolerated the police, just as a bull elephant does when he allows a small boy to drive him with a light stick." The simile, like most of West's figures, crystallizes the relationship and gives each part its proper weight.

Though the point has already been made, West proceeds to increase its power and to charge it with implication by his use of leitmotif. The image of the "torchbearers" has been loaded with such emotional force that what would otherwise have been a casual remark—"every other person one of his torchbearers"—is here a terrifying one.

At this point, West could have begun his long expository passage, for he has already set in motion a complex response by the image of the "torchbearers"; but before he does so, he chooses once again to dramatize the scene through action. This wish to propel the reader into the action before interrupting the scene seems to be West's way of committing the reader to follow him. By dramatizing the action first, he leads the reader to question why the action is significant—thereby increasing tension. When he does answer this unexpressed question, the answer not only increases the reader's understanding, it intensifies his expectation.

A close reading of the following passage, an expository one and a rather long one for West, will demonstrate the manner in which he is able to discard one source of tension while still seeming to increase the over-all tensity. West has already suggested so much about his "torchbearers" that when he explains them here at length, he produces an effect of psychological closure. At the same time that he is fulfilling one psychological need—the need to understand the origins of his torchbearers—and bringing the reader to rest on that level, he is, on another level, creating a new tension: the previously suggested capacity for violence in these people is now made manifest. The reader can only await the eruption with fascinated horror.

There is more to be revealed, however, in the passage than

such a transferal of tension; of equal importance is the style. One sees West's unique talent clearly at work here. The brute power of his monosyllabic words, the short poetic sentences, and the economy of expression are immediately apparent. No less obvious is the care with which West chooses his language. He seizes upon images that are precise, yet at the same time suggestive and emotionally loaded: they not only evoke the desired mood, they literally force it upon the reader. As the exposition develops, one sees that the images, the vague clichés, and the sentence rhythms are not only clever, they are brilliantly functional. The tone is sure; it captures the crowd's attitude and that of the author as well. The balance between the two is a fine one and is slightly ambiguous. Perhaps West's most effective device, here as elsewhere, is his use of the short terminal sentence. He finishes a train of thought—usually, but not necessarily, a paragraph—with a brutally blunt sentence that impresses itself so forcefully on the mind that the reader unconsciously continues drawing implications without actually being drawn up in his reading.

Beneath all runs West's unique, smouldering intensity, an intensity that seems to be due to the hammerlike economy of the language, but which goes beyond it, gathering momentum until it is on the verge of erupting into violence:

> New groups, whole families, kept arriving. He could see a change come over them as soon as they had become part of the crowd. Until they reached the line, they looked diffident, almost furtive, but the moment they had become part of it, they turned arrogant and pugnacious. It was a mistake to think them harmless curiosity seekers. They were savage and bitter, especially the middle-aged and the old, and had been made so by boredom and disappointment.
>
> All their lives they had slaved at some kind of dull, heavy labor, behind desks and counters, in the fields and at tedious machines of all sorts, saving their pennies and dreaming of the leisure that would be theirs when they had enough. Finally that day came. They could draw a weekly income of ten or fifteen dollars. Where else should they go but California, the land of sunshine and oranges?
>
> Once there, they discover that sunshine isn't enough. They get tired of oranges, even of avocado pears and passion fruit. Nothing happens. They don't know what to do with their time. They

> haven't the mental equipment for leisure, the money nor the physical equipment for pleasure. Did they slave so long just to go to an occasional Iowa picnic? What else is there? They watch the waves come in at Venice. There wasn't any ocean where most of them came from, but after you've seen one wave, you've seen them all. The same is true of the airplanes at Glendale. If only a plane would crash once in a while so that they could watch the passengers being consumed in a "holocaust of flame," as the newspapers put it. But the planes never crash.
>
> Their boredom becomes more and more terrible. They realize that they've been tricked and burn with resentment. Every day of their lives they read the newspapers and went to the movies. Both fed them on lynchings, murder, sex crimes, explosions, wrecks, love nests, fires, miracles, revolutions, wars. This daily diet made sophisticates of them. The sun is a joke. Oranges can't titillate their jaded palates. Nothing can ever be violent enough to make taut their slack minds and bodies. They have been cheated and betrayed. They have slaved and saved for nothing. (pp. 156-57)

The effectiveness of the scene comes as the result of many factors, "intensity" being among the most important. It is due to West's emotional involvement and, paradoxically, to his intellectual detachment; for without the latter, he would lack that control which focuses the power of the work by compressing it. It is owing to his world view and to various tensions within the work, to his economy, to his ability to create swift impressions, and to the grotesque quality of his work. If one were forced to single out the root of his intensity, one would probably turn to his imagery: violence is everywhere. The scenes in West's novels most clearly memorable—Miss Lonelyhearts butchering the lamb, Miss Lonelyhearts twisting the arm of the "clean old man," and the riot in *The Day of the Locust*—are all scenes of violence.

Regarding his technique in *Miss Lonelyhearts,* West wrote: "Violent images are used to illustrate commonplace events. Violent acts are left almost bare."[11] The remark is an illuminating one. It not only indicates the thought West put into his writing, it indicates the care with which he husbanded his language.

By such a method, West created an impression of ceaseless violence, and he did so without running the risk of extravagance, repetition, and monotony. In allowing violent acts to speak for themselves, he avoided the danger of overusing the verbal resources available to express violence and was thus able to employ them more effectively when he needed them. West was careful to follow his own dictum. "Violent images," for example, are used to describe Tod's reflections on Faye Greener and Homer Simpson's life together:

> After she had gone, he wondered what living with her would do to Homer. He thought it might straighten him out. He fooled himself into believing this with an image, as though a man were a piece of iron to be heated and then straightened with hammer blows. He should have known better, for if anyone ever lacked malleability Homer did. (*The Day of the Locust*, p. 101)

Again, when Shrike caresses Miss Farkis while sermonizing to Miss Lonelyhearts about sainthood, "His caresses kept pace with the sermon. When he had reached the end, he buried his triangular face like the blade of a hatchet in her neck" (*Miss Lonelyhearts*, p. 17). The opposite device is even less difficult to find. The passage describing the end of the cockfight in *The Day of the Locust* illustrates West's stark presentation of violent acts:

> Miguel freed his bird and gave the other back to the dwarf. Abe, moaning softly, smoothed its feathers and licked its eyes clean, then took its whole head in his mouth. The red was finished, however. It couldn't even hold its neck straight. The dwarf blew away the feathers from under its tail and pressed the lips of its vents together hard. When that didn't seem to help, he inserted his little finger and scratched the bird's testicles. It fluttered and made a gallant effort to straighten its neck.
>
> "Pit birds."
>
> Once more the red tried to rise with Juju, pushing hard with its remaining leg, but it only spun crazily. Juju rose, but missed. The red thrust weakly with its broken bill. Juju went into the air again and this time drove a gaff through one of the red's eyes into its brain. The red fell over stone dead.
>
> The dwarf groaned with anguish, but no one else said anything. Juju pecked at the dead bird's remaining eye. (p. 127)

In an article, "Some Notes on Violence,"[12] West presents some insights into his use of violence and his reasons for using it; but perhaps his most interesting comment is found in his article entitled "Some Notes on Miss L.": "A novelist can afford to be anything but dull. . . . I was serious therefore I could not be obscene. I was honest therefore I could not be sordid."[13] Only violence remained, and he used it to create one great image of ceaseless human suffering.

The impression of continual violence in West's work largely results from his figures of speech. Metaphors and similes abound in his work. When they are absent, West's style is no longer unique: it is merely fine writing in what Percy Lubbock calls "the dramatic mode"; but it is strangely un-Westian. Its vague resemblance to Hemingway's style is evident in the description of the cockfight and in a passage from the pastoral interlude in *Miss Lonelyhearts:*

> He sat smoking a cigarette, while she prepared supper. They had beans, eggs, bread, fruit and drank two cups of coffee apiece.
>
> After they had finished eating, there was still some light left and they went down to look at the pond. They sat close together with their backs against a big oak and watched a heron hunt frogs. Just as they were about to start back, two deer and a fawn came down to the water on the opposite side of the pond. The flies were bothering them and they went into the water and began to feed on the lily pads. Betty accidentally made a noise and the deer floundered back into the woods. (p. 88)

But such writing is extremely rare and is almost always used to counterpoint West's usual figurative style. The figures are sometimes strained and ineffective, as in the description of Homer's sobs: "The sound he made was like that of a dog lapping gruel" (*The Day of the Locust,* p. 32); often startling and grotesque: "When he swallowed, his neck bulged out and he made a sound like a miniature toilet being flushed" (*Balso Snell,* p. 18); sometimes characterizing, as when Homer describes Faye in terms appropriate to his character: "She was as shiny as a new spoon" (*The Day of the Locust,* p. 46); but almost always strikingly vivid. They have the personal stamp of the author upon them. More central to the present concern, however, is the power of West's imagery. As early as *The Dream Life of Balso Snell,* West revealed his ability to seize upon frightening images: "His Adam's apple was very large and looked as though it might be a soft tumor in his throat" (*Balso Snell,* p. 18). The work, however, is a pastiche. Only in his later major works do his images constantly force themselves upon the reader, and only there do his images seem to be an essential element of his style.

Sometimes the intensity of the imagery stems from the apparent casualness of delivery: "On most days he received more than thirty letters, all of them alike, stamped from the dough of suffering with a heart-shaped cookie knife" (*Miss Lonelyhearts,* p. 2); "the gray sky looked as if it had been rubbed with a soiled eraser" (*Ibid.,* p. 11). More often, however, the images arrest because they are original and so often touched with anger or pain: "He kneaded her body like a sculptor grown angry with his clay" (*Ibid.,* p. 55); "as he followed her up the stairs to his apartment, he watched the action of her massive hams; they were like two enormous grindstones" (*Ibid.,* p. 66); "a newspaper struggled in the air like a kite with a broken spine" (*Ibid.,* p. 11); "as he hobbled along, he made many waste motions, like those of a partially destroyed insect" (*Ibid.,* p. 107).

So fundamental are metaphor and simile to West's style that his descriptive passages—small and few as they are—are rarely realistic. As a consequence, they have a suggestive and emotional power disproportionate to their length. The effectiveness of many of West's descriptive passages is due to an expressionistic and surrealistic element of unreality about them. The result is a subtle and strange suggestiveness, as when Miss Lonelyhearts visits Betty:

> As they moved into the living-room, his irritation increased. She sat down on a studio couch with her bare legs under and her back straight. Behind her a silver tree flowered in the lemon wall-paper. (*Ibid.,* p. 28)

"Flowered" is charged with an ambiguity that is unnatural; an impression of movement is the result. It is this ability to create suggestive movement in the inanimate world which allows West to bring to reality a new dimension of life.

West seems to have taken great pleasure in playing with language, and as a result much of his work is experimental. He thought of himself as a comic, not a humorous writer. A study of his use of language for comic purposes bears out his judgment. While some of his stylistic experiments are connected with individual works, others, such as his use of jokes, burlesque, and cliché, are common to all.

There is a tendency at first glance to dismiss West's jokes as pubescent humor in bad taste. Such a view tends to ignore not only their abundance, their existence in every novel, but the element of conscious artistry in West. It would be possible to dismiss jokes such as "A hand in the bush is worth two in the pocket," in *Balso Snell* (p. 7), as a youthful manifestation of boisterous spirits; but one cannot dismiss so readily the existence of jokes such as the following one from *Miss Lonelyhearts:* " 'I am a great saint,' Shrike cried, 'I can walk on my own water' " (p. 16); or the joke put by Mary to Faye in *The Day of the Locust:* " 'Let him [Earle] ride a horse, he's a cowboy, ain't he?' " (p. 87) The cumulative effect of such jokes is scatological. By exploiting the inherent vulgarity of such jokes, West creates a revulsion from the physical in his readers. Not only does another joke in *The Day of the Locust* mirror man's bestiality, it is in such execrable taste that it almost acts as a social criticism—that tastelessness is the running sore of a sick society: " 'He [Earle] dassint [go home]. He got caught in a sheep car with a pair of rubber boots on' " (p. 69).

To a large extent, West's work is rooted in vulgarity. It was his precious ability to create miniature portraits of a society steeped in vulgarity. Only a writer with West's talent could deal esthetically with "two disembodied genitals" drawn on the walls of a telephone booth (*Miss Lonelyhearts*, p. 63). A mark of his inherent good taste was his ability to transcend the manifestations of that pervasive and sickening vulgarity. Much of this ability to temper the unsavoriness of his subject resulted from his pose of amused "detached observer of the ironies in the human struggle,"[14] and from a vision conveyed in comic idioms such as clichés.

John Sanford has noted West's "habit of speaking clichés in italics."[15] The same "in italics" effect occurs in his writing. Most prevalent in *The Dream Life of Balso Snell,* clichés are used in that work for destructive reasons, and, because iconoclastic, they are more robustly comic than in his later works. West used the cliché much as Shakespeare used the pun: at first merely a *jeu de mots,* it later was used to characterize, to reveal relationships, and to inject wry and dry comedy into his work. West became more expert in his use of the cliché as his work developed.

The exuberant spirit characteristic of West's early use of the cliché is most clearly seen in the Beagle Darwin passages and in the seduction scene at the end of *The Dream Life of Balso Snell:*

> Up into his giant heart there welled a profound feeling of love for humanity. He choked with emotion as he realized the truth of his observations. . . . (p. 55)
>
> . . . . .
>
> She was a fine figure of a woman. (p. 56)
>
> . . . . .
>
> No longer was she dry and sticklike, but a woman, warmly moist.
>
> They sat and devoured each other with looks. . . . (p. 57)

In *A Cool Million,* the spirit is much the same: "A widow well on in years"; "it was a humble dwelling much the worse for wear"; "our hero . . . was a strong, spirited lad. . . ."

If one juxtaposes the clichés found in Shrike's advice to Miss Lonelyhearts, or those found in Faye Greener's stories to Tod Hackett, one finds a great difference in tone, control, and subtlety, but little difference in essential satiric purpose. The satiric aim has not changed, but the depth and dimension of the satire has. In *The Dream Life of Balso Snell,* the satire is simple and comical. Irreverent and antiliterary, it is too bright and spirited to move the reader in any vital way. To a large extent, this failure is also the defect of *A Cool Million:* the satire, while serious, is so playfully presented that one is neither engaged nor enraged by it. The clichés fall too incessantly and too boisterously upon one's ears for him to examine them. The result is comic but basically self-defeating.

Miss Lonelyhearts is of a different order. When Miss Lonelyhearts attempts to reply to his letter writers, the reader is stunned, in the context of the novel, by the strident hollowness of his cant and clichés: " ' "The best things in life are free" ' " (p. 62); " 'Christ died for you. . . . His gift to you is suffering . . .' " (p. 95). The reader's response to Shrike's clichés is more ambivalent. Shrike's mocking advice—altered just enough to color the platitudes and make them interesting—is comic but so vicious in its intent and so frightening in its implication that one is forced to examine its content. This necessity for re-examining clichés—some of them the ones men live by—is one of the most disturbing aspects of West's art. It is part of what gives his work its personal quality and makes it a direct rather than a vicarious experience for the reader.

In *The Day of the Locust,* West does not, or is unable to, require such direct examination of one's beliefs. Instead, he uses clichés in a manner that forces the reader to re-examine his perceptions about people and about various aspects of life. How better to reveal the corrupting influence of pretense on one's emotions than to describe Harry Greener's responses in language deadened and made insincere by cliché? It seems that nothing but sustained analysis could so well reveal the falseness of his responses, the essential corruption of his real feeling; and yet the effect is terribly funny. The result, again, is one of tension in the reader. The clichéd response is comic, but its implications are not.

This shorthand method of characterization by cliché gives the novel an unusual air of substantiality. The characters, grotesque as they are and sketchy as their analysis is, seem, nevertheless, to suggest life and depth. The technique is basically a dramatic one: these passages are like dialogue that furthers the action of the story and at the same time reveals attitudes and states of mind. One of Faye Greener's stories shows how:

> A young girl is cruising on her father's yacht in the South Seas. She is engaged to marry a Russian count, who is tall, thin and old, but with beautiful manners. He is on the yacht, too, and keeps begging her to name the day. But she is spoiled and won't do it. Maybe she became engaged to him in order to spite another man. She becomes interested in a young sailor who is far below her in station, but very handsome. She flirts with him because she is bored. . . . She falls in love with him, although maybe she didn't realize it herself, because he is the first man who has ever said no to one of her whims and because he is so handsome. Then there is a big storm and the yacht is wrecked near an island. Everybody is drowned, but she manages to swim to shore. She makes herself a hut of boughs and lives on fish and fruit. It's the

> tropics. One morning, while she is bathing naked in a brook, a big snake grabs her. She struggles but the snake is too strong for her and it looks like curtains. But the sailor, who has been watching her from behind some bushes, leaps to her rescue. He fights the snake for her and wins.
>
> Tod was to go on from there. He asked her how she thought the picture should end, but she seemed to have lost interest. He insisted on hearing, however.
>
> "Well, he marries her, of course, and they've rescued. First they're rescued and then they're married, I mean. Maybe he turns out to be a rich boy who is being a sailor just for the adventure of it, or something like that. You can work it out easy enough."
>
> "It's sure-fire," Tod said earnestly. . . . (*The Day of the Locust*, pp. 62-63)

How much more devastating an indictment of romanticism than a direct attack! The shallowness, the escapism, and the hollow sentimentality are much more tellingly revealed than would be possible by direct exposition, and all by implication rather than description.

In these later major works, West has made of the cliché a thing of art. He has used it for reasons of subtlety; and by varying the language slightly, he has preserved all the echoes of the old while creating something new and original. The clichés are altered by the slightest of modifications, and by elevation of tone. Thus, as examples of the former method, West modifies the cliché "beggers can't be choosers" to "beggers couldn't be choosers" (*The Day of the Locust*, p. 60); "just for the hell of it" becomes "just for the adventure of it" (*Ibid.*, p. 63). The latter method is that used by Shrike. It consists of bathing the clichés in rhetoric, and of imaginatively corrupting literary echoes:

> "You are fed up with the city and its teeming millions. The ways and means of men, as getting and lending and spending, you lay waste your inner world, are too much with you. . . . So you buy a farm and walk behind your horse's moist behind, no collar or tie. . . ." (*Miss Lonelyhearts*, p. 78)

Closely related to such literary clichés is the "journalistic" cliché. West apparently relished burlesquing reviewers. The comic exaggeration of the following passage notwithstanding, the acuteness of West's ear is perceptible with amazing clarity:

> "At present I am writing a biography of Samuel Perkins. Stark, clever, disillusioned stuff, with a tenderness devoid of sentiment, yet touched by pity and laughter and irony. Into this book I hope to put the whimsical humor, the kindly satire of a mellow life.
>
> "On the surface *Samuel Perkins: Smeller* [for so I call it] is simply a delightful story for children. The discriminating adult soon discovers, however, that it sprang from the brain of a kindly philosopher, that it is a genial satire on humanity." (*Balso Snell*, pp. 32-33)

These journalistic clichés, which on the surface merely add a fillip to the humor, are really part of West's pervasive attack on a sick and shamming society. Their presence, no matter how comic, should alert the reader to the presence of social criticism. Further, in West's hands, the cliché facilitates economy and thereby, paradoxically, increases rather than diminishes his power.

West's vocabulary is, of course, admirably suited to this type of burlesque. William Carlos Williams, in an early article on West, "Sordid? Good God," discusses West's particular idiom and documents at length his central thesis that West's prose is peculiarly colloquial:

> Take it or leave it. It's impossible to quote effectively for anything but a minor purpose but that's approximately what the prose is like. It's plain American. . . . West has a fine feeling for the language. . . . Anyone using American must have taste in order to be able to select from among the teeming vulgarisms of our speech the personal and telling vocabulary which he needs to put over his effects. West possesses this taste.[16]

The danger that presents itself in any criticism of West's style is that one will fail to see the large number of passages of sheer poetry. In reading some of West's prose, such as the winter dancing scene from *Miss Lonelyhearts* which follows, one is reminded of D. H. Lawrence's remark that "the essence of poetry with us in this age of stark and unlovely actualities is a stark directness, without a shadow of a lie, or a shadow of deflection anywhere. Everything can go, but this stark, bare, rocky directness of statement, this alone makes poetry, to-day."[17]

> One winter evening, he had been waiting with his little sister for their father to come home from church. She was eight years old then, and he was twelve. Made sad by the pause between playing

> and eating, he had gone to the piano and had begun a piece by Mozart. It was the first time he had ever voluntarily gone to the piano. His sister left her picture book to dance to his music. She had never danced before. She danced gravely and carefully, a simple dance yet formal. . . . As Miss Lonelyhearts stood at the bar, swaying slightly to the remembered music, he thought of children dancing. Square replacing oblong and being replaced by circle. Every child, everywhere; in the whole world there was not one child who was not gravely, sweetly dancing. (*Miss Lonelyhearts*, p. 37)

If this is too lyrical to please—and it is too lyrical to be typical of West—one should be less concerned with the lyricism than with the rhythm. It is the short, rather balanced rhythm that is fine, that is subtle, that is Westian. But if this intellectually soft passage, which precedes Miss Lonelyhearts' being punched violently in the mouth, seems to be too atypical to demonstrate West's poetic style and rhythm, the following one—Faye Doyle's seduction of Miss Lonelyhearts—by its economy, tight near-iambic pattern, figurative language, and movement, is a better one, and an example of West's ironic style at its best:

> He smoked a cigarette, standing in the dark and listening to her undress. She made sea sounds; something flapped like a sail; there was the creak of ropes; then he heard the wave-against-a-wharf smack of rubber on flesh. Her call to him to hurry was a sea-moan, and when he lay beside her, she heaved, tidal, moon-driven. (*Ibid.*, p. 67)

IV. *The Dream Life of Balso Snell*

THERE IS A TENDENCY, because of its youthful exhibitionism, to dismiss *The Dream Life of Balso Snell* as an adolescent game, a clever and tricky tour de force written when West was twenty-two.[1] It is all this, but it is also much more. Despite its immature exuberance, self-conscious arty mannerisms, and sophomoric display of learning, *Balso Snell* has moments of brilliance. While West's style and ideas are refined later, and while his treatment of themes basic to his harsh, pessimistic world view are here couched in a bitter, self-defensive, adolescent *Weltschmerz*, his outlook and method undergo little appreciable change. This novel is the key to all his later works, for, in a sense, *Balso Snell* is an unconscious proclamation of influences and interests and, because so unsubtle, it is invaluable in understanding West's origins, thought, and style. Perhaps even more important, the novel allows us to perceive the essential unity of West's work. The influences upon the writer of *Balso Snell* were, almost without exception, the influences upon the writer of *Miss Lonelyhearts* and *The Day of the Locust*: French literature,[2] Jung and Freud, the Bible, Swift, Eliot and Joyce, Kafka, and Dostoevski.

Light has indicated West's tendency in the novel to satirize "his influences while he reflects them";[3] a rapid examination of the novel reveals the accuracy of this observation. In addition to the obvious satire of Dostoevski and Catholic mysticism, West satirizes (1) surrealistic faith in a greater self realizable by dreams: "Even though a man may remove himself from everyday reality to the point of absurdity . . . the simple truth is always the same: man is an animal";[4] (2) Freudian preoccupation with sexual fantasies and the subconscious; and (3) Joyce's artistic pretentiousness.[5] Moreover, always a highly imagistic stylist, in

Balso Snell West seems to parody his own style, to parody what Louis Aragon called " 'the vice called surrealism . . . the immoderate and passionate use of the drug which is the image.' "[6]

The general satiric intention of the novel is widely known. Perhaps no remark about it has been so much publicized, discussed, and accepted at face value as West's that *Balso Snell* was written "as a protest against writing books."[7] Thus Alan Ross has called it "a sneer in the bathroom mirror at Art—cocksure, contemptuous, well-informed and rejecting openly the object of its search";[8] Malcolm Cowley, "a joke" that "as a whole doesn't come off";[9] and Light, a "declaration" that "art is a private matter, best done when least understood."[10] The novel, as Light has suggested,[11] is also much more. West is not merely ridiculing art in the destructive fashion of the Dadaists, although in unmasking the sham implicit in art he is surely trying to do this in part. West's protest against writing books is as much a protest against the consequences of reading literture—the artificiality and sense of unreality, the self-consciousness and poisonous awareness that result from wide reading.

The theme of literary falseness *vs.* the truth of reality shares center stage with the following problem, simply stated: the world of books is an unreal world which paradoxically heightens man's awareness of the real world around him. It does so by giving him insight into the forces working upon his psyche as well as upon the world. Because of man's nature and the nature of the world, the result of this insight is either escapism or a tortured, inhibiting self-consciousness. He becomes so aware of the forces at play upon him that he falls, in his attempt to escape this knowledge, into a treacherous pattern of self-deceit. Wide reading forces him constantly to evaluate his behavior and to compare himself and others to literary figures. He grows to interpret—or misinterpret—himself solely in literary terms. In an attempt to escape from the facile automatic label, he is driven to assume subtle and devious poses. The poses are inevitably self-conscious but necessary if one is to preserve one's sense of originality or the integrity of one's ego. The entire process leads, paradoxically, to distortion rather than to clarity of vision; one loses sight of what he and others really are. Baldly stated, and oversimplified here, the problem of awareness of reality is a somewhat more complicated problem and one which, with variations and with the exception of *A Cool Million*, West never quite puts down.

If he deals here with such problems in a playful manner, it is probably because he lacked emotional and artistic control; and perhaps the influence of Paris contributed its share to the boisterous formlessness of the novel. Light has indicated how much of *Balso Snell* has its roots in Dada:

> Disgust, anti-intellectualism, and glorification of the physical man are important aspects of Dada, and all are central to *Balso Snell.* The most important influence is Dada's anti-intellectualism, for more than anything else *Balso* is a hysterical, obscure, disgusted shriek against the intellect. This world of the mind is the cause of man's misery, for here dreams are born. The misery and frustration come when man finds, as he must, that dreams are lies; and this realization in turn leads to that desire to shatter and to destroy which is found in so many of West's cheated and embittered creatures.[13]

If West in his later novels transcends his Dadaistic origins by giving his despair a formal coherence impossible in the shapeless nihilism of Dada, he nevertheless begins where they began—with the contemptuous destruction of art; and it is this aspect of *Balso Snell* which first captures the attention.

West begins his attack with the opening lines: "While walking in the tall grass that has sprung up around the city of Troy, Balso Snell came upon the famous wooden horse of the Greeks. A poet, he remembered Homer's ancient song and decided to find a way in. . . ." (p. 3) The irreverent tone has been struck: even the ancients are not sacred.

In typical fashion, West heaps allusion upon allusion, enveloping all in scatological ridicule:

> On examining the horse, Balso found that there were but three openings: the mouth, the navel, and the posterior opening of the alimentary canal. The mouth was beyond his reach, the navel proved a cul-de-sac, and so, forgetting his dignity, he approached the last. O Anus Mirabilis! (p. 3)

The last remark, probably a pun on Dryden's poem, reveals how playful, allusive, and comprehensive the attack is. The game of juggling titles, names, and meanings has begun, and the work continues, a sustained burlesque of authors, works, and literary conventions. Thus, the prayer that shortly follows: "O Beer! O Meyerbeer! O Bach! O Offenbach! Stand me now as ever in good stead!" (p. 4) is a boisterous parody of Stephen Dedalus' final words in *A Portrait of the Artist as a Young Man* and, at the same time, a burlesque of the invocation to the muse. The archaic style, in keeping with the subject matter, is continued throughout this section. As always, West is careful to adapt his style to the subject. However, with a genius for incongruity, he constantly uses anticlimax and cliché for comic effect.

Thus, when burlesquing the epic catalog, he builds up an arithmetical climax: "Balso immediately felt like the One at the Bridge, the Two in the Bed, the Three in the Boat, the Four on Horseback, the Seven Against Thebes" (p. 4). The humor of the catalog stems not only from its pedestrian numerical ascent, but from the movement as well: from the sublime to the ridiculous to the sublime; from Horatius at the bridge, he moves to copulation—stopping off by the Four Horsemen of the Apocalypse—then to the Seven against Thebes. The movement is not accidental: West has deliberately stopped with an example of exalted courage. The cliché that follows, with its juxtaposition of high and low, drops the reader from this pinnacle with a calculated thud: "And with a high heart he entered the gloom of the foyer-like lower intestine. The cliché (and, at the same time, the ridicule of the cliché) that follows strikes the comic chord of literary sacrilege that West wants to establish: "To keep his heart high and yet out of his throat, he made a song" (p. 4).

The irreverent juxtaposition of scatology and religious allusion in the song shocks the reader, but the song is so wretched—not even doggerel—that he is not sobered by it. The names given to the song are burlesques both of long titles and of dual ones. While vaguely appropriate, they show evidence of strain. The occasional awareness that West is striving for effect mars the novel. Once West has established the tone, he is compelled to try to sustain it, and because the demands of doing so are too great, he fails.

Perhaps an even greater failing is West's indiscriminate inclusiveness. The work rambles and falters because West has alluded to, and attempted to ridicule, too much. More dangerous to his purpose is the possibility that the allusions will bewilder the reader or the possibility that the reader will be distracted by trying to unscramble the allusions. Both are fatal to whimsical literary burlesque. Once effort is expended to decipher the joke, it is no longer much of a joke. Moreover, when so many allusions occur, many are bound to be unfamiliar to the average and even the well-read reader. The novel then becomes a game: sometimes one recognizes the allusion, and sometimes one does not.

This defect becomes more and more prominent in the conversation with the guide. The list of names dropped within less than two pages is staggering: C. M. Doughty, George Moore, Daudet, Ingres, Picasso, James, Bergson, and Cézanne. West is, of course, satirizing "arty" conversations or artistic pretension, but satire of this sort is effective only if the reader feels comfortable; and generally he feels comfortable only when recognition is not difficult. Such fragile humor would be more effective if the allusions were not integral parts of one's understanding of the humor but merely enriched the humor. However, the opposite is true frequently enough to be disturbing. When, for example, the religious mystic, Maloney the Areopagite (a turn on Dionysius the Areopagite), remarks that "it is only necessary to remember Leda and Europa" (p. 11), what must those who have never heard of them feel? Or those who have only heard of them? Nothing.

This tendency to build allusions—often esoteric ones—into the foundation of his novel is not restricted to *Balso Snell; Miss Lonelyhearts* and *The Day of the Locust* are also highly allusive works. In those novels, however, the allusions are functional and subdued, poetic and obscurely symbolical.

If this aspect of West's artistry makes him a difficult writer, and *Balso Snell* a difficult book, there are numerous other humorous aspects of the novel which are less dependent on the reader's recognition. The reader can appreciate the numerous clichés without knowing that some are parodies of classical and Renaissance literature, or without recognizing the echo which is being called up. Sometimes the echo is not literary but is one drawn from vulgar folklore. When this is the case, the echo is usually so striking that it is difficult not to catch it. At the end of the "Life" of St. Puce, there is a witty example:

> "I think you're morbid," he said. "Don't be morbid. Take your

> eyes off your navel. Take your head from under your armpit. Stop sniffing mortality. Play games. Don't read so many books. Take cold showers. Eat more meat." (p. 13)

A large number of people—at least a large number of men—will recognize the advice to "take cold showers" to be the advice given to people who desire to remain continent. Some, thinking of a more sordid situation, will recognize it as the advice given to young boys to stop masturbating. The calculation of giving this advice to a religious mystic in order to "cool off" his religious ardor juxtaposed with its conventional use lends humor although it is perhaps too shocking to be effective with some readers.

There are, however, numerous examples of juxtaposition less likely to offend. More than any other device, it seems to be the mainstay of West's comic technique in *Balso Snell.* Basically, it is the surrealist art of incongruity, of yoking dissimilar images together: "Balso . . . came upon a man, naked except for a derby . . . who was attempting to crucify himself with thumb tacks" (p. 10); "the hot sun of Calvary burnt the flesh beneath Christ's upturned arm making the petal-like skin shrivel until it looked like the much-shaven armpit of an old actress" (p. 12). In yoking the sublime and the ridiculous and creating an effect of anticlimax, West counts upon the element of surprise one feels at being so abruptly dropped. The surprise due to grotesque incongruity is funny, but West has a tendency to overwork the trick until the reader is so prepared for it that he is surprised not to find it.

West must have sensed this, for as the novel progresses, he drops his early, rather facile use of juxtaposition and enriches it by injecting a new note of satire. Thus, even when the simpler form of juxtaposition is present, it serves a purpose. After reading "The Pamphlet," Balso begins to reflect:

> In his childhood, things had been managed differently; besides, shaving had not been permitted before the age of sixteen. Having no alternative, Balso blamed the war, the invention of printing, nineteenth-century science, communism, the wearing of soft hats, the use of contraceptives, the large number of delicatessen stores. . . . (p.31)

This Swiftian juxtaposition of the possible and the ludicrous reduces social comment to the ridiculous. West here, as so often elsewhere, is trying to ridicule something out of existence—in this case, a scapegoat for the evils of the world.

But even this technique lacks real comic vigor; only when West selects an object of satire and dramatizes it in concrete images does his comic talent assert itself. When West culminates his attack on art and satire of the "smart, sophisticated, sensitive yet hard boiled, art-loving frequenters of the little theatres" (p. 30), he leaves a grotesque but penetrating picture of pretense and affectation:

> In case the audience should misunderstand and align itself on the side of the artist, the ceiling of the theatre will be made to open and cover the occupants with tons of loose excrement. After the deluge, if they so desire, the patrons of my art can gather in the customary charming groups and discuss the play. (pp. 30-31)

Much of the force of West's satire and humor is due to his ear for language. There is something just right about the phrase, "can gather in the customary charming groups." It suggests much more than it states: clever brochures, arty little theaters, and intermission "tea or coffee" in the foyer. The tendency to open new realms of implication by a careful control of tone and the echo phrase is one of West's great assets. It adds a felt but unstated dimension to his work and particularly to the various episodes in *Balso Snell.*

This ability to create layers of implication and connotation is most evident in the long seduction speech at the end of *Balso Snell.* Aside from the satiric importance of several of the arguments, in focusing an analysis on one sustained passage, one discovers an amazing degree of thought and subtlety of construction:

> (1) Here Balso threw himself to the ground beside his beloved.
>
> (2) How did she receive him? At first by saying no.
>
> (3) No. No! Innocent, confused. Oh Balso! Oh Balso! with pictures of the old farm house, old pump, old folks at home, and the old oaken bucket—ivy over all.
>
> (4) Sir! Stamping her tiny foot—imperative, irate. Sir, how dare you, sir! Do you presume? Down, Rover, I say down! The prying thumbs of insolent chauffeurs. The queen chooses. Elizabeth of England, Catherine of Russia, Faustina of Rome.

(5) The two noes graded into two yes-and-noes.

(6) No . . . Oh . . . Oh, no. Eyes aswim with tears. Voice throaty, husky with repressed passion. Oh, how sweet, sweetheart, sweetheart, sweetheart. Oh I'm melting. My very bones are liquid. I'll swoon if you don't leave me alone. Leave me alone, I'm dizzy. No . . . No! You beast!

(7) No: No, Balso, not tonight. No, not tonight. No! I'm sorry, Balso, but not tonight. Some other time, perhaps yes, but not tonight. Please be a dear, not tonight. Please!

(8) But Balso would not take no for an answer, and he soon obtained the following yesses:

(9) Allowing hot breath to escape from between moist, open lips: eyes upset, murmurs love. Tiger skin on divan. Spanish shawl on grand piano. Altar of love. Church and Brothel. Odors of Ind and Afric. There's Egypt in your eyes. Rich, opulent love; beautiful, tapestried love; oriental, perfumed love.

(10) Hard-bitten. Casual. Smart. Been there before. I've had policemen. No trace of a feminine whimper. Decidedly revisiting well-known, well-plowed ground. No new trees, wells, or even fences.

(11) Desperate for life. Live! Experience! Live one's own. Your body is an instrument, an organ or a drum. Harmony. Order. Breasts. The apple of my eye, the pear of my abdomen. What is life without Love? I burn! I ache! Hurrah!

(12) Moooompitcher yaaaah. Oh I never hoped to know the passion, and sensuality hidden within you—yes, yes. Drag me down into the mire, drag. Yes! and with your hair the lust from my eyes brush. Yes . . . Yes . . . Ooh! Ah! (pp. 60-61)

In keeping with the entire *carpe diem* tone of the passage, West continues his archaisms in creating a transition between the Renaissance and the present. "His beloved" is an archaism which, while genuine during the Renaissance, is ironic today. There should be no ambiguity in this irony, and yet ambiguity remains because the word acts as a bridge between two ages: the past and the present are blended in one word.

The past is immediately discarded in the next line: "How did she receive him? At first by saying no." The reader seems to be in the full-blown present, but the third paragraph, beginning with Mary McGeeney murmuring, "No. No! Innocent, confused. Oh Balso! Oh Balso!" presents echoes of the eighteenth-century distressed heroine of Richardson and Fielding. With the heavy-handed humor of the statements that follow, the reader reaches the American frontier, "with pictures of the old farm house, old pump, old folks at home, and the old oaken bucket—ivy all over." Again, there are incongruous echoes, but the mainstream of the satire, still focused on Mary McGeeney's protests, remains a satire of the sentimental heroine. The entire notion of the virtuous maiden (trapped in the clutches of a horrid villain?) is being attacked as a shabby fraud.

As the fourth paragraph begins, the emphasis still is on the plight of the sentimental heroine: "Sir! Stamping her tiny foot—imperative, irate. Sir, how dare you, sir! Do you presume?" How telling a blow, the "tiny foot"! And how mannered the stylistic tendency to state simply the manner of inflection: "imperative, irate." The alliteration compounds the artifice. Yet, in the next sentence, the reader is brought crashing down to the present with all its vulgar, sordid echoes as Mary cries, "Down, Rover, I say down!" Although still apparently in the present in the next line, "the prying thumbs of insolent chauffeurs," the reader hears an echo, as in the poetry of T. S. Eliot, and hence is made uncomfortable. The line stirs him, and should, for an idiotic association has been made. Comparing the line with one from *Hamlet*—"the slings and arrows of outrageous fortune"—one finds that their meter is almost identical. And because "insolent chauffeurs" recalls "insolence of office," the association with Hamlet's "to be or not to be" soliloquy is reinforced. The allusion is suggestive. The comparison of Mary McGeeney with Hamlet is as absurd as that between Prufrock and Hamlet, and to introduce the element of suicide here would be sheer madness. Desperation, despair, and indecision are all recalled, but transplanted to Miss McGeeney, they become farcical. Her suggested desperation is made false by the surroundings; her despair, melodramatic; and her indecision, unreal. Other aspects of the passage echo Eliot. Like Eliot, West uses myth and allusion to create universality; and as Eliot, in *The Waste Land,* moves from high society to low life, so does West.

Paragraph six brings the world of the "true romance" of pulp fiction. The cheap emotion and obvious eroticism are captured by West's striking feeling for clichés. But as he ends the paragraph, he moves the reader out of the unreal world of pulp fiction into a world closer to the one the reader knows. The real world, presented here with irony and humor, is still seen by West as full of sham. In representing the love game in such crude fashion, he touches on something sordid and ugly.

Already a pattern has been established: the alternation of romanticism and realism. It is continued in paragraphs nine and ten. By abruptly following the lush first passage with the hard-bitten second, West enlarges the focus of his literary satire. In the first passage, the exoticism of a Pierre Louys is being attacked; in the second, the crisp, cynical approach of modern pulp magazine realists. At the same time, he is satirizing the consequences of reading literature. By touching his passages of full-throated passion with a perverted romanticism or with a cynical worldliness, he reveals the corrupting power of literature: genuine feeling is no longer possible.

West has also introduced a new subjective element. He has moved away from the objective world (paragraphs two through eight) to focus his attention on the subjective world. In the early paragraphs, he is interested in contrasting what seems to be with what is; in the two later paragraphs, he is concerned not with what is but with what is desired. The choice he presents is distorted, and the entire sequence makes for a savage indictment of life and of literarily induced aspirations.

The last paragraph is, of course, a parody of the final monologue in Joyce's *Ulysses*. Drawing upon a knowledge of Molly Bloom, one is able to fill in his picture of Mary McGeeney. The result is a rather complex reader response: is West suggesting that "once brought down to earth" every woman—even the shamming intellectual one—will whimper an "earthy" yes?

There is a danger, in reading this episode, that one will forget it does not occur, that it is a dream, that it is the figment of Balso's imagination. It is important that one does not, for in this realization lies one of West's hidden jokes. Balso's very dreams have been corrupted by literature. When he dreams, even a wet dream, it is a literary one and one which reveals a desire to embrace all experience. Just as diverse reading is an attempt vicariously to experience all things, so, in this dream, Mary McGeeney becomes all things. First, she is the sentimental heroine—a tender morsel to titillate one's delicate fancy. But the habits of reality intrude—just for a moment, in the line, "Down, Rover, I say down." She then becomes a series of historical personages known for great love affairs. This phase passes, and she becomes the liquid, yearning, impassioned stereotype of the pulp magazines; the yielding, swooning female of cheap pornographic literature; the unreal product of a disturbed imagination. The habits of reality, however, intrude once again in vivid fashion. A sordid back-seat seduction is vicariously relived. Then, swiftly spinning, the reader enters the world of the Middle Eastern *femme fatale.* Opulent decadence is the theme. Reality again intrudes, but this time with literary overtones. She is now the violent, hungry whore, the nymphomaniac who exhausts and discards men after a brutal, silent sexual combat. Then erotic and excited echoes float past Balso's mind in broken fragments, turning at the end to the disjointed sexual moan that ends *Ulysses.*

There is nothing more to experience. All the ages, all the types have been experienced; and if only in a dream, this is no less important. The inclusiveness of the dream reflects the desire for variety, the jaded and perverted palate of the dreamer. After this, who can be satisfied with the fractional possibility that any single woman can offer? Thus the sexual theme of West's attack reaches its climax. Literature and sexual maladjustment have been fused and are linked together in a fundamental fashion. The last grotesque twist has been given to the consequences of reading literature.

The episode, as indeed the entire novel, is marred by an occasional lapse of taste or control. Thus, the "Hurrah!" at the end of the eleventh paragraph is gratuitous and disturbing. Enough is going on to fascinate and amuse so that this playful addition is out of key. West's youthful exuberance once again impresses the reader as just that, and by drawing attention to itself, fails as art. The novel, however, is more than an uneven literary game. It is a comic statement of serious themes. It would be wrong to assume that West is not serious in his concern with such themes as self-consciousness and sexual maladjustment merely because he distorts and toys with them. The measure of this concern is revealed by how little the themes change in his later works.

The natural tendency to overlook the novel's themes is due to its tone and emphasis. Unlike West's later novels, which have larger social, political, or philosophical relevence, *Balso Snell* is more personal. Hidden beneath an esthetic nihilism is an analysis of "the disintegration of Self, and its illusion of superiority at its most pathetic moment of neurotic isolation."[14] There is also much more; for while *Balso Snell* undoubtedly contains numerous passages of scarcely disguised autobiographical analysis, West's ironic and self-conscious temperament forced him to generalize his self-analysis, to make it applicable to the body of mankind. Thus, when West undertakes an analysis of the central theme of the novel—the disparity between illusion and reality—he draws from his own psychic experience because in doing so he is able to lay bare the problem and to deal with it more economically, more comprehensively, and from various perspectives. But West is not interested in his personal eccentricities. Though there is a sense in which the parody is personal exorcism, the brunt of the satire is directed outward in order to unmask the artifices of man and civilization: "Basically, West was always a sociological writer, moved by the horrible emptiness of mass lives; and in this sense all his books are indictments, not so much of economic systems, but of life itself."[15]

The novel's satiric overtones—and the novel is also more than a literary satire—should suggest a measure of West's social consciousness; for there is a sense in which satire is impossible out of a social context. However, in the main, the preoccupations—or more correctly, the treatments—remain personal and adolescent. Always prone to an episodic style, in no other novel does West make of the episode a formless end in itself. That he does select such an episodic method, with all its advantages—and disadvantages—of plot, story line, temporal dimension, and character development, indicates that West's involvement was such that he wanted to take up various aspects of life illustrative of his theme without the added burden of creating a unified work of art. By choosing the "picaresque" format, he was able to concentrate on his message; and all of the episodes reflect his belief that illusions —resulting as they do from naïve idealism—at best offer no escape, and more often than not are destructive: hence, in his later novels, the destruction of Miss Lonelyhearts, Lemuel Pitkin, and Homer Simpson. The format of *Balso Snell* allows West constantly to take up an illusory ideal, examine it, satirize it, and then reject it.

The classical ideal comes under attack first and is immediately dispatched by sheer scatological irreverence. West lingers a moment to satirize the commercialization of culture, in the form of the guide with "Tours" embroidered on his cap, and modern vulgarity, in Balso's response to "a beautiful Doric prostate gland": "Doric, bah! It's . . . simply an atrophied pile" (p. 6). Fleeing from this grotesque apostle of culture, Balso comes upon the religious ascetic, Maloney the Areopagite. He is merely the second in a long line of grotesques West creates in an attempt to reveal the sordid reality underlying the false gods of Art, Religion, and Culture: the basic motive, as West sees it, being "the attraction of the female" (p. 26).

The method is still the same—indignity through irreverent association. The tale of "St. Puce" renders such a line as the following absurd: "And I must remind you, you who plead a puce too small physically, of the nature of God's love and how it embraceth all" (p. 11). The archaism "embraceth," echoing the King James Bible, compounds the insult. Indeed, the entire episode, a broad, eye-winking parody of the Incarnation, Passion and Eucharist, serves to ridicule the Catholic church and, by implication, religion in general. Before closing the episode, West hits upon the already mentioned device—happily suited to his purpose—of treating religion as if it were a weakness or a vice, suggesting that religion is an unnatural state of mind curable by a conscious act of the will.

This is the last of the sneering dismissals. The remainder of the novel is spent in dealing with psychological problems which, if West had treated them differently, are not totally divorced from reality. But the problems are so grotesquely distorted that for all West's fine insight into them, the reader is led, as West intends, to dismiss their relevance. By destroying a problem, he destroys any possible solution. This is a rather facile form of nihilism, but it serves his purpose—that of unmasking sham and illusion.

In this respect, John Gilson's "*Crime Journal*," if read, or capable of being read, seriously, has much in it that is real and provocative. The problems in it dealing with reality, identity, and the irrational, are, however, deliberately made absurd by West's "sexualizing"[16] rather than spiritualizing his treatment; and yet when Dostoevski, West's favorite author, treats them they are not absurd. Instead of exempting Dostoevski from attack, his profound treatment of the human condition on the contrary places him in the front rank. West's attack is not only a tribute to Dostoevski's art but to the relevance of his analysis. How better to destroy art and meaningful problems than to cut down a giant who handled such problems artistically! Yet, such indirect attack is not enough for West; as so often in *Balso Snell,* he must pull the rug completely out from under his readers. He does so in the following exchange between John Gilson and Balso, unmasking the entire journal as a sham written for the most unexalted reason. At the same time, West hopes to accomplish two destructive results: he hopes to oppose "psychology" and "art" or, in other terms, to separate the real from the artificial, and to show how unimportant art really is in daily life, and how ugly is its true reason for existing:

> "Well, nosey, how did you like my theme?" . . .
>
> "Interesting psychologically, but is it art?" . . .
>
> "What the hell do I care about art! Do you know why I wrote that ridiculous story—because Miss McGeeney, my English teacher, reads Russian novels and I want to sleep with her. . . .
>
> ". . . But I'm fed up with poetry and art. Yet what can I do. I need women and because I can't buy or force them, I have to make poems for them. God knows how tired I am of using the insanity of Van Gogh and the adventures of Gauguin as can-openers for the ambitious Count Six-Times. And how sick I am of literary bitches. But they're the only kind that'll have me. . . ." (pp. 23-24)

Whether West believed that art existed, baldly stated, in order to "attract the female" even at the time that he was writing *Balso Snell* is debatable. It is possible that this is merely another example of his desire to shock by bringing problems down to their most primitive and universal level; but one should be cautious of a facile dismissal: both *Miss Lonelyhearts* and *The Day of the Locust* emphasize the sexual origins of human behavior.

The mocking self-consciousness, sneering self-analysis, and sexual debunking of John Gilson's diary is carried over to "THE

PAMPHLET" and made its sole purpose for existence. Again it is as if West were trying to push introspection to its extremity and thereby render it absurd. This theatric sense of absurdity is not a passing phase in West's development. It is the rock on which he built all his novels. It merely seems to loom larger in *Balso Snell* because of the novel's formlessness and because his method, in this work, is one of direct attack rather than indirect implication. Instead of placing his characters in situations which reveal futility and absurdity, as he does in *Miss Lonelyhearts* and *The Day of the Locust,* West in this work makes the characters and their very problems absurd. The problems raised in *Balso Snell* are treated in a fashion calculated to create this effect. One has, and is meant to have, the feeling that these are not problems that one can take seriously. This response is vastly different from one's feelings about the problems in *Miss Lonelyhearts.*

West is able to accomplish this effect in *Balso Snell* not by dealing with trivial problems as opposed to those dealt with in *Miss Lonelyhearts* and *The Day of the Locust,* but by choosing banal or unbelievable incidents to dramatize the problems. Add the element of melodrama to banalty or incredulity and one creates a problem that is a farce not worthy of serious consideration. The technique is quite simple. "THE PAMPHLET" immediately presents a traditional theme. Proustian variations on memory and experience to one side, the basic theme is that of the onslaught of time. Such a theme is a respectable one and has been treated respectably. West, however, will have none of it:

> Yesterday, while debating whether I should shave or not, news of the death of my friend Saniette arrived. I decided not to shave.
>
> Today, while shaving, I searched myself for yesterday's emotions. Searched, that is, the pockets of my dressing gown and the shelves of the medicine closet. (p. 24)

The opening debate, "To shave or not to shave?" when expressed in those terms is banal, but it is also suggestively (and perhaps deliberately) mocking a literary classic. The melodramatic "news" of the death of his "friend Saniette" (already made laughable by the juxtaposition with the previous debate) appears to tip the scales. The reader is to assume, but can hardly take seriously, the implication that Balso fails to shave because he is despondent. What can one think of a grief that endures one day but that it is absurd? By selecting a trivial example of grief (neglecting to shave) and by speeding up the time element (one day), West has made the reader laugh at the entire problem, a problem that, treated differently, would be a moving one.

The technique briefly sketched out here appears throughout *Balso Snell.* Along with ridicule, it is West's favorite means of preventing the reader from a serious consideration of the problem at hand. It seems clear, however, that West wants the reader to realize that he is undermining the validity of a problem, for his ridicule often consists in drawing attention to that very problem. This is done by caricaturing it.

The entire sequence in "THE PAMPHLET" between Saniette and the narrator is so insistent in its presentation of neurotic dishonesty and incompatibility in human relationships that if one were oriented toward deriving insights from it, one could. On the whole, one does not because West has been so lavish with comparison.

> Only a portion of my dislike for Saniette is based on the natural antipathy pessimists feel for optimists, cowboys for Indians, cops for robbers. For a large part it consists of that equally natural antipathy felt by the performer for his audience. My relations with Saniette were exactly those of performer and audience. (p. 25)

Removing the numerous farcical and satiric examples and toning down the language, the situation is one of great suggestive power. Once the "cowboys for Indians" and "cops for robbers" illustrations—provoking as they do an element of farce in the rest—are removed, for example, the "performer" and "audience" images take on a metaphoric power suggestive of psychological rather than theatrical relationships.

These same points made about "THE PAMPHLET" can be made elsewhere, particularly in the Beagle Darwin letters, with little difficulty. One would like to think that the entire technique demonstrates West's fine ear and the fragility of his tone in *Balso Snell.* On the contrary, it seems to suggest the opposite. The humorousness of the method, while often effective, is not subtle and not difficult to achieve; moreover, it is not an intrinsic part of his expression. For all the unique images and striking comparisons, for all the grotesque brilliance of much of the writing, the humor lacks the fundamental unity of that in *Miss Lonelyhearts* or *The Day of the Locust.* In those works, it is almost impossible to separate the writing into its various serious, pathetic, and comic-satiric parts. That one can do this so readily in *Balso Snell* suggests the accuracy of what has already been thought: the work is marred by contrivance, immature display, and a desire to shock.

The literary variety of *Balso Snell* can best be explained in similar terms. Interspersed throughout the novel are an invocation, one song, two poems, a saint's life, a journal, a pamphlet, two letters, a passage in dramatic form, and a final oration.[17] The literary classifications that are not covered by these labels fall into the province of style where, as has already been pointed out, West tries to be as comprehensive in his experimentation. All that has been suggested about West's stylistic and literary parody, about his allusions and echoes, indicates that from beginning to end *Balso Snell* is a sustained attack against art.[18] West's premise (perhaps but not necessarily a deliberately shocking one) that literature tends to produce an inhibiting and neurotic self-consciousness led him to make such an attack. The consequences are spelled out in the following passage:

> You once said to me that I talk like a man in a book. I not only talk, but think and feel like one. I have spent my life in books; literature has deeply dyed my brain its own color. This literary coloring is a protective one—like the brown of the rabbit or the checks of the quail—making it impossible for me to tell where literature ends and I begin. (p. 47)

Throughout the novel the pattern of attack is varied: sometimes it consists of showing that life is terrible and literary attempts at pretending it is not are illusory; sometimes, as in the following examples, West is merely contrasting literary language with vulgar reality, attempting to show how literature colors and beautifies one's vision of life, and how lyrical outbursts fade before harsh reality:

> Feeling his lips on her forehead, Janey Davenport, [the Lepi] gazed out over the blue waves of the Mediterranean and felt the delight of being young, rich, beautiful. . . . Now she knew the

> thrill she had never known before . . . had found it in the strength of this young and tall, strangely wise man, caught like herself in the meshes of the greatest net human hearts can know: Love.
>
> Balso took her home and, in the hallway of her house, tried to seduce her. . . . When he began to unbutton, she said with a desperately gay smile. . . . (pp. 38-39)
>
> . . . . .
>
> . . . he saw standing naked before him a slim young girl busily washing her hidden charms in a public fountain. . . .
>
> She called to him, saying:
>
> "Charge, oh poet, the red-veined flowers of suddenly remembered intimacies—the foliage of memory. Feel, oh poet, the warm knife of thought swift stride and slit in the ready garden. . . .
>
> Throwing his arms around her, Balso interrupted her recitation by sticking his tongue into her mouth. But when he closed his eyes to heighten the fun, he felt that he was embracing tweed. He opened them and saw that what he held in his arms was a middle aged woman dressed in a mannish suit and wearing horn-rimmed glasses. (pp. 31-32)

Despite the variations, the theme always remains recognizable.

In the pages following these passages, West uses Miss McGeeney's description of Samuel Perkins to attack biographies and to ridicule the notion of compensation, symbolism, the theory of correspondences, in particular, and literary periods. The central attack, however, seems to be on the ability of literature—and literary language—to render the pedestrian poetic. In Perkins, the biographer of E. F. Fitzgerald, the biographer of D. B. Hobson, who in turn is the biographer of Boswell, whose fame rests on his biography of Johnson, West in an absurd fashion has presented a literary nonentity and, by implication, mediocrity in a rather pure form. Miss McGeeney's biography transforms him into a giant. The point: if literature can work such a transformation, it can perpetrate any fraud.

The Perkins passages again reveal a favorite theme in *Balso Snell*: the ugly motives for which literature is written. Here, the motive is a vain desire for a vague immortality; later, West reduces this to a simple wish for recognition: "The wooden horse, Balso realized as he walked on, was inhabited solely by writers in search of an audience . . ." (p. 37). By adding these motives to the sexual one, West has made of the artist a petty person. The grand function of the artist thus becomes a fraudulent one.

It is interesting that all of the inhabitants of the horse are writers with the exception of the guide. West seems to be making a statement about human nature: not that all people are writers or would-be writers, but that all people—with the exception of those who exploit them—are performers. It is, however, a subtle form of gymnastic that they perform.

With no talent—and no one in *Balso Snell* has any—the characters nonetheless must create. They do this by telling stories about themselves, their psychology or their life. But in the telling self-aggrandizement occurs, and melodrama and absurdity result. Each character, as well as art, is thereby made escapist, but escapist via the vehicle of self-dramatization. By means of these unlovely and unloved grotesques, West seems to be revealing the need of all men to render a harsh, unpleasant existence significant. By dramatizing their lives, they give beauty, excitement, and meaning to an otherwise ugly, dull, and trivial existence. The dream motif, always at the center of West's later work, already finds its way there in his first novel.

In his treatment of the dream motif, West is concerned not merely with esthetic illusion but with the very artifices of Western civilization: Religion, Culture, "Home and Duty, Love and Art" (p. 61). It is vital that we perceive this truth about the novel, for it is also a truth about all of West's novels; in every one West is obsessed with analyzing the illusions by which men make life bearable. Light, though pointing out that "dreams are lies," has chosen to emphasize the "search for a dream" without sufficiently pointing out West's ruthless annihilation of each dream. "The search for a dream to believe in" may be "right,"[19] but it is also impossible. The very dream, whether it be the "Christ dream" of *Miss Lonelyhearts,* the "American dream" of *A Cool Million,* or the "Hollywood dream" of *The Day of the Locust,* is a pathetic, comic, tragically absurd illusion. Every episode in *Balso Snell* is but a reworking of this theme—the prevalent reality of almost every one being physical or sexual. It is no accident that for all the talk of art, religion, and culture, this short novel (less than sixty pages) contains several sexually hard up young men, a homosexual, a sadistic, sexually motivated beating, "tons of loose excrement" falling on theatergoers who fail to prefer "animal acts" to Art (pp. 30-31), a couple of *ménage à deux,* two seductions—one attempted, one performed—and two orgasms, the last one closing the novel.

Just prior to the last episode in the novel, West, donning the mask of B. Hamlet Darwin, introduces a variation on the novel's central theme which he is to develop at great length in *Miss Lonelyhearts.* It is "the tragedy of all of us": the disparity between men's spiritual aspirations and their physical reality:

> "Who among us can boast that he was born three times, as was Dionysius? . . . Or who can say, like Christ, that he was born of a virgin? Or who can even claim to have been born as was Gargantua? Alas! none of us. Yet it is necessary for us to compete . . . with Dionysius the thrice born, Christ son of God, Gargantua. . . . You hear the thunder, you see the lightning, you smell the forests, you drink wine—and you attempt to be as was Christ, Dionysius, Gargantua! You who were born from the womb, covered with slime and foul blood, 'midst cries of anguish and suffering.
>
> "At your birth, instead of the Three Kings, the Dove, the Star of Bethlehem, there was only old Doctor Haasenschweitz who wore rubber gloves and carried a towel over his arm like a waiter.
>
> "And how did the lover, your father, come to his beloved? [After a warm day in the office he had seen two dogs in the street.] Did he come in the shape of a swan, a bull, or a shower of gold? No! But with his pants unsupported by braces, came he from the bath-room." (p. 55)

In *Miss Lonelyhearts,* West treats man's spiritual aspirations with tenderness and classic simplicity; he understates rather than overstates man's need to dramatize his existence. In the presence of such restrained pathos, laughter is difficult, but in *Balso Snell* what makes the reader laugh—and, as always in West, it is an anxious, uneasy laugh, even if a loud one—is precisely the absurd length to which the characters carry this self-dramatizing tendency. Everywhere the tellers charge their tale with vital significance: a flea becomes a saint; a schoolboy's infatuation produces a "tortured Russian journal"; an unknown and unspeakably mediocre biographical subject becomes an inspirational genius and a source of immortality; a sordid Parisian affair that ends in pregnancy becomes a great betrayal and the source of infinite introspective delicacy; and so it goes. Of such stuff are dreams made; and from such stuff do men build the drama of their lives.

Such distortion of reality is, of course, nonsense; and in *Miss Lonelyhearts,* West plays contrapuntal changes on the themes of *Balso Snell*: literary deceit becomes epistolary honesty; the self-aggrandizement, self-mockery; the over-all movement of the novel and of each episode from fantasy to sexual reality becomes in *Miss Lonelyhearts* a movement from sexual reality to fantasy. Only the concern with seeing man unmasked of illusion remains constant in West's work. But somehow West is no longer able to shriek with laughter at the unmasking, at his vision. The shriek keeps breaking into a sob.

V. Miss Lonelyhearts

STANLEY EDGAR HYMAN has called *Miss Lonelyhearts* "one of the three finest American novels of our century";[1] though an extreme claim, it is not a foolish one. A small, apparently simple novel with a very hard finish, *Miss Lonelyhearts* is West's masterpiece and the novel that most clearly reveals his singular sensibility. In no other novel are the tragic, comic, pathetic, and satiric so inseparably fused; in no other novel has he so nicely balanced the three emotional attitudes which are reflected in his novels—compassion, contempt, and suffering; and in no other novel has he developed such complex harmonies of meaning—harmonies resulting from the counterplay of the literal and the symbolical. Strident and garish as it is, *Miss Lonelyhearts* is a novel most delicately poised between agonizing pessimism and ironic amusement. It was a balance too fine for West to achieve in any other novel. Perhaps he achieved it in *Miss Lonelyhearts* because in it he first gives voice to violent despair and because, though it is his most personal, subtle, and important philosophic statement of life, it followed too soon after *Balso Snell* to escape that novel's broad comic irony.

Though clearly unique among West's novels, *Miss Lonelyhearts* reflects little change in West's world view; in retrospect, one sees much in *Balso Snell* that foreshadows the novel. Thus, in addition to the dream, search, isolation, and communication—or lack of communication—themes; the conflict between illusions and reality; self-dramatization; the analysis of man's spiritual nature; and the similarity between Shrike, Miss Lonelyhearts, John Gilson, and Beagle Hamlet Darwin, there are verbal echoes: the "*Anima Christi*" in *Balso Snell* becomes Shrike's prayer to Miss Lonelyhearts, the jokes at the expense of religion in *Balso*

Snell are paralleled by Shrike's numerous ones, the murder of the idiot with a knife parallels the murder of the lamb both descriptively and in its psychosexual implications, and the staginess of John Gilson and B. Hamlet Darwin's speech is echoed constantly in Shrike's and occasionally in Miss Lonelyhearts'. But if some of the devices are old, the artistry is new.

By polishing and artistically reworking themes dealt with in his earlier experimental novel, West begins a pattern that applies as well to *A Cool Million* and *The Day of the Locust.* It is as if he had to experiment once before he discovered the vehicle which would artistically sustain his concern. More important, it suggests that West's anxieties persisted until they were resolved esthetically. *The Dream Life of Balso Snell–Miss Lonelyhearts* and *A Cool Million–The Day of the Locust* form pairs; hence, after the completion of *Miss Lonelyhearts,* and presumably after *The Day of the Locust,*[2] West tended to seek out a new conceptual center. Thus, despite certain prevalent motifs in all four novels, the first two are personal, psychological, and philosophical; the latter two, more social-psychological and political. Moreover, the second novel in each pair treats the problem in a darker, less comic fashion. The skepticism and nihilism that found such personal and boisterous expression in *Balso Snell* is in *Miss Lonelyhearts*, muted but intensified and made moving by its more serious treatment. The vision, however, has changed little. One errs if he fails to see this fundamental truth merely because in *Balso Snell* West aroused laughter, and in *Miss Lonelyhearts* the laughter is "too deep for tears." It is not the problem that determines one's response, it is the treatment.

Unlike the picaresque formlessness of *Balso Snell*—a construction admirably suited to comedy—structurally *Miss Lonelyhearts* has a composition similar to that of tragic drama. In its movement from ignorance through experience to discovery—a movement similar to that in *Balso Snell*—it approximates Francis Fergusson's "tragic rhythm of action . . . Purpose, Passion (or Suffering) and Perception."[3] The purpose: to answer the letters; the passion: Miss Lonelyhearts' agonizing realization of the reality of human suffering; the perception: his vision of God and his acceptance of Him. West, however, does not tell the whole story of Miss Lonelyhearts; one never sees him in his "innocent" state. Instead, the novel concentrates on the last weeks of his life, thereby crystallizing the reader's impressions into a single one of enormous power.

Even more dramatic in technique is West's use of discovery and reversal; perhaps here it will help to draw parallels. In most conventionally structured modern drama, the nature of the problem is presented as soon as possible; the first act curtain rarely rings down before it is clearly known. West proceeds to do the same thing and does it with stunning brilliance. Within two pages after the novel begins, and certainly within twelve, the nature of Miss Lonelyhearts' problem is quite clear: how does he answer the letters when the letters are "no longer funny"?

In the second and third acts of this kind of dramatic structure, the protagonist struggles to resolve his problem. This struggle usually consumes most of the stage action; and in *Miss Lonelyhearts,* the bulk of the novel is concerned with Miss Lonelyhearts' struggles to escape, to find an answer that will ease his readers' suffering and his own. The dramatist, in constructing his play, is constantly trying to create suspense as to how the protagonist will resolve his problem. He does this by delaying the resolution, which is usually achieved by a discovery and a reversal, as long as possible. An attempt is made by the dramatist to have his discovery and reversal come as near to the end of the play as possible.

One can see such a structural pattern in Maxwell Anderson's play *Winterset.* Mio's problem in the play is how to revenge his father. Suspense is built up by the difficulty of the task. One wonders whether Mio will kill his father's murderers or be killed. Late in the third act, Miriamne informs him that he should not seek revenge, for his father would surely have forgiven them. This is a new and startling discovery for Mio, and an immediate reversal follows. Mio's humanity reasserts itself; he no longer desires revenge. This significant change is intended to increase his stature. Death, however, follows swiftly, and in five minutes the play is over.

In like manner, West delays Miss Lonelyhearts' discovery until the last fifteen or twenty pages of the novel. It is a gradual, groping, uncertain realization, but this merely increases the tension and the reader's interest. Only two pages before the end is the final ironic "discovery" made that "Christ is life and light." The reversal is instantaneous; "his identification with God was complete" and his acceptance total. Death follows three hundred words later and the "tragedy" is ended.[4]

What is important about *Miss Lonelyhearts* is the superimposition of comedy upon its tragic structure. It cannot be insisted too strongly that if one is to use such terms, in a sense inappropriate ones, *Miss Lonelyhearts* is a comedy with tragic overtones rather than a tragedy with comic overtones. In reality, these terms lose their meaning when discussing a novel such as *Miss Lonelyhearts:* is Beckett, to name another apostle of the absurd, writing a tragedy in *Waiting for Godot* or a comedy? Horace Walpole's remark that "the world is a comedy to those that think, a tragedy to those who feel" fails utterly to describe West's peculiar sensibility. It does, however, help illuminate West's "unified sensibility," and by extension, that of many other exponents of the Absurd.

Whatever one may think of the novel, it is clear that it is not a conventional tragedy; not merely because Miss Lonelyhearts lacks tragic stature—he is fundamentally heroic in conception if not in execution—but because the very fabric of the novel is invaded by comic irony and incongruity.[5] Thus, despite a natural wish to read *Miss Lonelyhearts* as moral, even Christian, tragedy, one can only do so by doing violence to West's pessimistic belief that life is without discernible order or meaning.

Divergent readings are inevitable, for, contrary to appearances, *Miss Lonelyhearts* is not a simple or "easy" novel. Perhaps it is misread more often than not. An article by James F. Light offers a characteristic example:

> These letters ask the eternal question of crippled humanity: "What is the whole stinking mess for?" To the question Miss Lonelyhearts can find no answer. He therefore must try to find the true Christ. By the end of the novel Miss Lonelyhearts has, through the negation of his personality, gained a mystical union with God and the peace that comes with grace. But to the contemporary materialistic world, Miss Lonelyhearts has become hysterical, become "sick.". . . The moral is obvious. Only through the perfect love of Christ can the pain of man be alleviated; only through faith can the conflict between the evil in the universe and

> the goodness of God be reconciled. Christ gave these answers; the letters have forced Miss Lonelyhearts to them. But just as the world of Christ was not ready, so the world of today is still unready.[6]

Light is not quite so unequivocal in his major study of West; but despite his recognition that West doubted Christ's divinity, his reading changed but little:

> Miss Lonelyhearts is shot by Doyle, destroyed, like Christ, by the panic and ignorance of those whom he would save. Doyle, and in him suffering man, shatters the only solution to the intolerableness of man's pain, destroys the Christlike man who perceives that love and faith are the only answers to man's pain in a universe he cannot understand.
>
> True belief in the Christian answers, however, rest upon the dissolution of the self and the subsequent mystical experience of God's love and grace. . . . After God's love and grace, the personal ecstacy they bring is a "reality," but the reality is incommunicable.[7]

Such a reading attempts to make a Christian of West, something very difficult to do for more than one reason. But even more disturbing, such a reading is diametrically opposed to everything West believed. It offers a solution to the human dilemma when it is clear that West had none and never attempted to pose one. Moreover, one cannot so read the novel without ignoring West's finest achievement—his control of irony.

Even on the purely narrative level, as distinct from the various symbolic ones, ironies permeate the novel. They begin on the first page:

> The Miss Lonelyhearts of The New York *Post-Dispatch* (Are-you-in-trouble?— Do-you-need-advice?— Write-to-Miss-Lonelyhearts-and-she-will-help-you) sat at his desk and stared at a piece of white cardboard.

Not only is the Miss an uncertain Mr., but soon, even before realizing the source of his suffering, one learns that, besides being incapable of helping anyone, Miss Lonelyhearts is badly in need of help himself:

> Although the deadline was less than a quarter of an hour away, he was still working on his leader. He had gone as far as: "Life *is*

> worth while, for it is full of dreams and peace, gentleness and ecstacy, and faith that burns like a clear white flame on a grim dark altar." But he found it impossible to continue. The letters were no longer funny. He could not go on finding the same joke funny thirty times a day for months on end. And on most days he received more than thirty letters. . . . (p. 2)

Miss Lonelyhearts is tortured by two questions: Why doesn't God make manifest the higher order which governs man's existence? And, if there is no higher order—if God does not exist—how does one respond to suffering and injustice in this world?

The problem of man's response to suffering is raised in the first chapter. West ironically counterpoints Miss Lonelyhearts' platitudes about life's being beautiful with sordid reality. In three letters, he captures the essence of a pervasive, inexplicable human suffering that afflicts guilty and innocent, pious and impious alike; and in response to the letters, Miss Lonelyhearts has to fight "himself quiet."

While there is little irony in the letters, just as in *Balso Snell*, much of West's commentary in *Miss Lonelyhearts* is developed by means of ironic contrasts and associations. Perhaps *Miss Lonelyhearts* is West's greatest work because in it the ironies are the most subtle and the most poetically conceived. Sometimes they are simple ironies intended to point out the impossibility of communication, to show that hell is other people. Hence the incompatabilities that permeate the novel: Shrike the "satyr" wedded to Mary, who has been fighting to remain a virgin ever since she married; tortured Miss Lonelyhearts, whose "confusion was significant," paired with Betty, whose "order was not"; and crippled Doyle, who is "all dried up" and "isn't much" in bed, married to Fay Doyle, who is insatiable.

At other times, the ironies are merely verbal, as when West conveys how Miss Lonelyhearts, in desperation to escape, will clutch at any straw: "although he had tried hot water, whiskey, coffee, exercise, he had completely forgotten sex" (p. 45). It is one of the novel's cruelest ironies that sex actually does lead him out of the world, not, however, in the way he thought it would. For just as Oedipus' act ultimately led him out of the city, Miss Lonelyhearts' problem leads him to withdraw, but not with Betty to the country: the withdrawal is a catatonic one.

Once aware that "'the majority of the letters are profoundly humble pleas for moral and spiritual advice, that they are inarticulate expressions of genuine suffering . . . [Miss Lonelyhearts] is forced to examine the values by which he lives. This examination shows him that he is the victim of the joke and not its perpetrator'" (p. 76). The ironic depth of this joke is fearful, for Miss Lonelyhearts is not a godless man seeking faith: that search is altogether too trivial and trite. He is a fallen man who would seek a reassuring word from God. The horror of *Miss Lonelyhearts* proceeds from one's awareness of how Miss Lonelyhearts has fallen and of the agony of his fall. In his naked need to embrace God, this "son of a Baptist minister" (p. 6) arouses genuine pity and terror. Miss Lonelyhearts—this man in whom "something secret and enormously powerful" stirred when "he shouted the name of Christ" (p. 20)—is West's modern (fallen) Myshkin, West's "holy fool." He is the first and most memorable of West's scapegoats. The symbolic cry that rings throughout the novel is the loud cry of Christ crucified, "My God, my God, why hast thou forsaken me?" (Matt. 27:46) From the beginning, Miss Lonelyhearts realizes that "Christ was the answer, but, if he did not want to get sick, he had to stay away from the Christ business. Besides, Christ was Shrike's particular joke" (p. 6).

Shrike is a bird of prey. Again and again he impales Miss Lonelyhearts on the barbed edge of his rhetoric. "'The same old stuff,'" he remarks upon reading one of Miss Lonelyhearts' columns. "'Why don't you give them something new and hopeful?'" (p. 7) In passages full of the brilliant puns, clichés, and rhetoric in which West excelled, he cruelly and systematically destroys one of Miss Lonelyhearts' potential escapes after another: first, "the soil" (". . . you turn up the rich black soil, the wind carries the smell of pine and dung across the fields and the rhythm of an old, old work enters your soul"); then, "the south seas" ("You live in a thatch hut with the daughter of the king. . . . Her breasts are golden speckled pears, her belly a melon" . . .); then the pursuit of pleasure ("You fornicate under pictures by Matisse and Picasso, you drink from Renaissance glassware, and often you spend an evening beside the fireplace with Proust and an apple"); and finally, just before "the First Church of Christ Dentist" ("Father, Son and Wirehaired Fox Terrier"), art:

> Tell them that you know that your shoes are broken and that there are pimples on your face, yes, and that you have buck teeth and a club foot, but that you don't care, for tomorrow they are playing Beethoven's last quartets in Carnegie Hall and at home you have Shakespeare's plays in one volume. (pp. 78-83)

Calling Christ "the Miss Lonelyhearts of Miss Lonelyhearts," he relegates Christ to the same meaningless class as Miss Lonelyheart. As a result, the ivory Christ nailed to Miss Lonelyhearts' wall with large spikes fails to stir: "Instead of writhing, the Christ remained calmly decorative" (p. 19).

Miss Lonelyhearts tries to escape by ridiculing the problem out of existence. " 'Ah, humanity . . .' " he says mockingly. "But he was heavy with shadow and the joke went into a dying fall. He tried to break its fall by laughing at himself" (p. 10). That West is intent on demonstrating Miss Lonelyhearts' disintegration as a result of his search is early made apparent, for he describes Miss Lonelyhearts' desire to believe in Christ in the terrifying snake image of insanity.

Hoping by association to regain a sense of order, he seeks out Betty. Yet, she cannot console him; for the more desperate, helpless, and alone he feels, the more hostile and violent he becomes: " 'I've got a Christ complex,' " he shouts. But his shouts are accompanied by "gestures that were too appropriate, like those of an old-fashioned actor" (p. 29). They are not completely false, but are no longer simple and true; introspection, self-consciousness, and isolation have corrupted his emotions: even in counterfeit responses he cannot escape from his fallen state.

" 'What's the matter sweetheart?' " he asks, again burlesquing the mystery of feeling at its source. " 'Didn't you like the performance?' " (p. 30) He is sick; and, unable to free himself from the cause of his sickness, he tries to revenge himself for the suffering he is undergoing. His revenge manifests itself childishly like that of his friends in Delehanty's who "did not know how else to revenge themselves" (p. 35). "Like Shrike, the man they imitated, they were machines for making jokes" (p. 36).

Again he seeks out Christ: "If only he could believe in Christ . . . then everything would be simple and the letters extremely easy to answer" (p. 63). But he cannot believe; Shrike has not allowed it. Instead, "Shrike had accelerated his sickness by teaching him to handle his one escape, Christ, with a thick glove of words" (pp. 78-79).

The country interlude with Betty further hastens his disintegration, for there he learns that nature does not cleanse. A vision of Eden changes nothing in the Bronx slums; he discovers this fact as soon as he returns:

> When they reached the Bronx slums, Miss Lonelyhearts knew that Betty had failed to cure him and that he had been right when he had said that he could never forget the letters. He felt better, knowing this, because he had begun to think himself a faker and a fool. (p. 93)

Once Miss Lonelyhearts acknowledges that "he could never forget the letters," all avenues of escape are cut off to him but Christ. His disintegration is swift. He reads one long, incredibly horrifying letter by "Broad Shoulders" and is in ruins within a week. Striving for humility, he dodges Betty "because she made him feel ridiculous" (p. 105). Unable to shake her innocence—she still lives in a Connecticut Garden of Eden—and unable to play at house any longer, he must avoid her. Miss Lonelyhearts' catatonic escape has begun; Shrike has cut off all others.

The withdrawal is foreshadowed by the number of times West refers to Miss Lonelyhearts' search for Christ as an escape. Moreover, as will be illustrated more clearly later, the abnormal nature of the withdrawal is built into the novel's imagery. Not only is the hollowness of his solution ironically suggested by the rock that he becomes, but the escapist nature of his "rocklike" tranquility is counterpointed against the true immersion of oneself in the sea of human suffering: "What goes on in the sea is of no interest to the rock" (p. 128). Further, if the description of Miss Lonelyhearts standing naked—indifferent to Shrike and four others—carefully examining "each cracker before popping it into his mouth" (p. 125) is not enough to point out his growing loss of contact with reality, one has only to note the way West refers to Miss Lonelyhearts' plans for the future—to get a new job and marry Betty—as "a castle in Spain" (p. 137).

Miss Lonelyhearts is sick because any affirmation of traditional values—represented in a soft and pure form by Betty—makes him feel absurd, and because he can discover no other values by which to live. He cannot accept Betty's world, a world in which she is a "party dress" and he is "just what the party dress wanted him to be: simple and sweet, whimsical and poetic, a trifle collegiate yet very masculine" (p. 136).

The scenes with Betty, amusing as they are, are genuinely poignant. They temper the novel's stridency, and they supply it with some of its warmth and tenderness, with a bittersweet suffering which contrasts sharply with the sordid and grotesque suffering of the letter writers. It is the novel's most heartbreaking irony that Betty's patient and innocent efforts to retrieve Miss Lonelyhearts make her pregnant and ultimately destroy him; for her final visit, apparently to plan "their life after marriage," by cutting off the cripple's escape results in his death. As in *Oedipus Rex,* the ironies are bitter ones: innocence and good intentions are not enough.

Such a literal reading of the novel, though satisfying to many readers and probably favored by most, ultimately fails to illuminate the novel's peculiar resonances. The novel seems to, and does, contain deeper symbolic and ironic reverberations. Some of these symbols and ironies are indicated in West's explanation of what he was trying to do in the novel:

> Miss Lonelyhearts became the portrait of a priest of our time who has a religious experience. His case is classical and is built on all the cases in James' *Varieties of Religious Experience* and Starbuck's *Psychology of Religion.* The psychology is theirs not mine. The imagery is mine. Chapt. I—maladjustment. Chapt. III—the need for taking symbols literally is described through a dream in which a symbol is actually flashed. Chapt. IV—deadness and disorder; see Lives of Bunyan and Tolstoy. Chapt. VI—self-torture by conscious sinning: see life of any saint. And so on.[8]

The "portrait" is an ironic one, but it is not strange that the irony should go unnoticed, or that West's description of Miss Lonelyhearts as "a priest of our time" should trigger stock responses of respect and compassion in the reader. West obviously wished to elicit such responses, for he takes pains to make clear Miss Lonelyhearts' priestlike role at several points in the novel. The note is struck early:

> On seeing him [Miss Lonelyhearts] for the first time, Shrike had

> smiled and said, "The Susan Chesters, the Beatrice Fairfaxes and Miss Lonelyhearts are the priests of twentieth-century America." (p. 7)

The metaphor is repeated again and again in various remarks by Shrike and then finally crystallized in the image describing Miss Lonelyhearts as he listens to the cripple's disjointed, abused outburst: "Like a priest, Miss Lonelyhearts turned his face slightly away" (p. 110). West, however, goes further and develops the character of Miss Lonelyhearts as a Christ figure. This identity, as well as the central theme of the novel—man in search of God—is suggested on the first page by the parody of the "*Anima Christi*" or "Soul of Christ" from Loyola's *Spiritual Exercises:*

> *"Soul of Miss L, glorify me.*
> *Body of Miss L, nourish me*
> *Blood of Miss L, intoxicate me.*
> *Tears of Miss L, wash me.*
> *Oh good Miss L, excuse my plea,*
> *And hide me in your heart,*
> *And defend me from mine enemies.*
> *Help me, Miss L, help me, help me.*
> *In saecula saeculorum. Amen."* (p. 1)

Lest the reader miss the point, on page six West thrusts upon him the image of a lamp post piercing Miss Lonelyhearts "like a spear," an image so obvious that he cannot ignore it. And, at the end, Miss Lonelyhearts is shot, with his arms "spread," ready for the martyrdom.

Throughout the novel, West continues the theme of man in search of God and uses Christian images to suggest Miss Lonelyhearts' emotional state. He is, at the same time, trying to indicate Miss Lonelyhearts' preoccupation with Christ and the impossibility of finding Him in this modern age. But this quest is merely part of the irony. Not only must the reader never forget *Miss Lonelyhearts*' link with *Balso Snell*—that "rejection of . . . the spiritual pretensions of man"—he must never forget that the Miss Lonelyhearts *are* the priests of his time.

"God," Nietzsche said metaphorically, "is dead";[9] and with Him, West adds, died the priest. In his place has arisen that peculiarly modern corruption, the advice columnist—the new father confessor and pastoral guardian. So essential to West is his readers' awareness of the identity of this modern debasement that he feels compelled to have Shrike establish the *equation* of twentieth-century priest to traditional priest seven pages after the novel begins: "'the Susan Chesters . . . are the priests of twentieth-century America.'" Only by recognizing the true identity of the subject in the portrait can one dissociate the novel from certain prevalent prejudices and preconceptions.

Christianity has lost its vital center; as a viable force it is dead. As he has before, and as he will again later, West here seizes upon an image or an objective correlative—Miss Lonelyhearts or his like—to symbolize the corruption in the palace of religion and, therefore, in the society. The religion Gibbon charged with causing the decline of the Roman Empire is itself declining, and with it—though not because of it—the West. In essence, Miss Lonelyhearts becomes an archetypal symbol of the decline of the West. The vision is Spenglerian to be sure, but one for which West had a great affinity, as Light points out:

> As Spengler and Valery had suggested (and West had read their criticisms), man's "progress" is leading to the end of Western civilization. West agreed with such viewpoints, though perhaps more emotionally than intellectually.[10]

The materialistic nature of that "progress" and West's hatred of it are revealed again and again, as Light also points out. (Significantly, Chief Satinpenny in *A Cool Million* refers specifically to Spengler and Valery in his diatribe against Western civilization.)

As a result of his Spenglerian vision and religious skepticism, West is placed in the paradoxical position of debunking religion while using the decline of Christianity to symbolize the decline of the West. On the surface, it appears to be an impossible task; closer examination reveals a logical, but no inherent, artistic contradiction. West's opposition, if one can use so strong a word, to Christianity is doctrinal or theological, not ethical. Moreover, West is not lamenting the decline of Christianity as much as he is using that decline as an archetypal symbol of the decline of Western civilization.

It seems impossible to explain the novel's peculiar reverberations without turning to the complex texture established by interweaving a comic and a tragic vision of Miss Lonelyhearts and Western society. Much of one's failure to sense the bitter comic irony of the novel results from the mythic conception of the novel and from West's capacity to feel compassion for basically unlovely types. Thus, despite his purpose—to analyze ironically Miss Lonelyhearts' "religious experience"—West is able to charge Miss Lonelyhearts with such genuine anguish that the reader is overwhelmed with compassion. One should not be led by a tender response to Miss Lonelyhearts' *angst* to ignore the novel's comic aspects, for in addition to, or maybe as part of, its symbolic intention, the novel is a case study of a modern Oedipus. West has taken a "classical" case history—an Oedipus complex—and, by the use of brilliant imagery, translated it into a work of art.

Stanley Edgar Hyman has neatly described Miss Lonelyhearts' Oedipus complex:

> Terrified of his stern religious father, identifying with his soft loving mother, the boy renounces his phallicism out of castration anxiety—a classic Oedipus complex. In these terms the Shrikes are Miss Lonelyhearts' Oedipal parents, abstracted as the father's loud voice and the mother's tantalizing breast. The scene at the end of Miss Lonelyhearts' date with Mary Shrike is horrifying and superb. Standing outside her apartment door, suddenly overcome with passion he strips her naked under her fur coat while she keeps talking mindlessly of her mother's death, mumbling and repeating herself, so that Shrike will not hear their sudden silence and come out. Finally Mary agrees to let Miss Lonelyhearts in if Shrike is not home, goes inside, and soon Shrike peers out the door, wearing only the top of his pajamas. It is the child's Oedipal vision perfectly dramatized; he can clutch at his mother's body but loses her each time to his more potent rival.[11]

The tidiness with which Hyman is able to describe Miss Lonelyhearts' complex is evidence of West's success. He was not, of course, trying to keep the complex or Miss Lonelyhearts' latent homosexuality a mystery.

The parallels between the two Oedipuses are striking: like Oedipus of old, this modern Oedipus tries to ease the suffering of his subjects; like him, he engages in a quest which ultimately and ironically results in the discovery of his true identity. However, as is to be expected of a modern Oedipus, the problem of identity is a sexual one: "who am I?" becomes "what am I?" Finally, both Oedipuses are scapegoats. In addition, there are numerous other parallels; for though comic in execution, Miss Lonelyhearts is heroic and archetypal in conception. With but one exception (the national figure—but really, scarcely even there, for Miss Lonelyhearts is a widely known figure to his readers), the following remark applies about as well to one as to the other:

> the hero is traditionally and historically a national figure, who is willing to subordinate his individual concerns for the larger good of the community. At the outset he is a free agent, who either by choice or special election, is gradually caught up in a chain of causality. He must assume the burden of the quest through which he meets and conquers the dragon that oppresses and blights the land. The regeneration of civilization may be the result of his success.[12]

There is no twentieth-century dragon, though there is a shrike; but nevertheless, the land is blighted:

> As far as he could discover, there were no signs of spring. The decay that covered the surface of the mottled ground was not the kind in which life generates. Last year, he remembered, May had failed to quicken these soiled fields. It had taken all the brutality of July to torture a few green spikes through the exhausted dirt.
>
> What the little park needed, even more than he did, was a drink. (pp. 9-10)

The theme of a parched earth in need of water occurs repeatedly:

> A desert, he was thinking, not of sand, but of rust and body dirt, surrounded by a back-yard fence on which are posters describing the events of the day. Mother slays five with ax, slays seven, slays nine. . . . Inside the fence Desperate, Broken-hearted, Disillusioned-with-tubercular-husband and the rest were gravely forming the letters MISS LONELYHEARTS out of white-washed clam shells, as if decorating the lawn of a rural depot. (p. 59)

West's vision of the people who populate this wasteland does not alter in his last three novels. The apocalyptic riot that ends *The Day of the Locust* is foreshadowed in *Miss Lonelyhearts* in the shattered letter writers and in a furtive glimpse of Tod Hackett's "torchbearers":

> Crowds of people moved through the street with a dream-like violence. As he looked at their broken hands and torn mouths he was overwhelmed by the desire to help them, and because this desire was sincere, he was happy despite the feeling of guilt which accompanied it.
>
> He saw a man who appeared to be on the verge of death stagger into a movie theater that was showing a picture called Blonde Beauty. He saw a ragged woman with an enormous goiter pick a love story magazine out of a garbage can and seem very excited by her find. (pp. 93-94)

The echoes from Eliot's *Waste Land* have already suggested that the novel is a moving modernization of the Grail legend. Perhaps only the solidity and intensity of West's vision have prevented the recognition that the world of *Miss Lonelyhearts* is the fallen world of myth. Adam and Eve in Eden are glimpsed in the pastoral interlude, but in the context of the novel, it is an unreal Eden. Betty, unconscious of the symbolic curse that afflicts the land, is not burdened with the mysterious, mythic sense of guilt that troubles Miss Lonelyhearts. At this mythic level, Betty seems to symbolize the restorative feminine principle in nature. Under her urging, after Miss Lonelyhearts' illness, they plan to take a trip to Connecticut.

> She told him about her childhood on a farm and of her love for animals, about country sounds and country smells and of how fresh and clean everything in the country is. She said that he ought to live there and that if he did, he would find that all his troubles were city troubles. (p. 77)

First they convalesce at the zoo: "He was amused by her evident belief in the curative power of animals. She seemed to think that it must steady him to look at a buffalo" (p. 86).

Betty's mythic function exists mainly to punctuate ironically Miss Lonelyhearts' failure, the exact nature of which can only be explained by perceiving the myth and the novel as an organic whole. While the main elements of the Grail legend are familiar—the wasteland, Fisher King, quest, lance and Grail—only a close, somewhat technical examination of the mythic parallels in the novel will reveal the brilliance of West's achievement. West, who probably knew Jessie L. Weston's work[13] on the Grail legend more than casually (he was probably introduced to it through

Eliot), seems to have felt free to depart from Miss Weston's interpretation when he found it useful. Thus, despite Miss Weston's convincing argument for a ritualistic rather than a Christian reading, West makes use of both interpretations; while the quest for the Grail is interpreted sexually, the Fisher King is not a life or fertility symbol so much as Christ, the "King of the Fishermen."

The novel's mythic characteristics begin at once. From the parody of the "*Anima Christi,*" it is apparent that Miss Lonelyhearts is on a quest, the precise nature of which is as vague as the original. One soon realizes it is to give "the dead world . . . a semblance of life . . . [by] bringing it [Christ] to life" (pp. 20-21). The parallels with Miss Weston's description of a variant of the Grail quest are clear. In both, the hero is oppressed by a sense of urgency; in both, he understands neither the nature of the task nor how to perform it; in both, there is the insistence upon the sickness of the Fisher King; in both, there is a suggestion that the death of the Fisher King is the "direct cause of the wasting of the land";[14] and in both, "the task of the Quester [is] that of restoring him to life."[15]

Though West has occasionally departed from Miss Weston's interpretation in adding other mythic elements to the central Grail quest, he seems to have followed her closely. Miss Weston connects a procession or nature ritual—a "resuscitation ceremony"—with the Grail legend: "The Vegetation Spirit appears in the song as an Old Man, while his female counterpart, an Old Woman, is described. . . ." In a note, Miss Weston adds: "besides the ordinary figures of the Vegetation Deity, his female counterpart, and the Doctor, common to all such processions, we have Phallus, Frog, and Horse."[16] The parallels of this ritual with the chapter "Miss Lonelyhearts and the Clean Old Man" are ingenious but unmistakable.

Miss Lonelyhearts and Ned Gates, alias Havelock Ellis and Krafft-Ebing (obvious surrogates for the doctor), encounter a "clean old man" who, as a homosexual, is not only a "defunct Vegetation Spirit"[17] but one who will serve to suggest his female counterpart as well. In his avowed purpose "to help," *i.e.*, to revitalize the old man, Miss Lonelyhearts' behavior parallels an early preliterary version of the Gawain variant: "he [Gawain] played the *role* traditionally assigned to the Doctor, that of restoring to life and health the dead, or wounded, representative of the Spirit of Vegetation."[18]

Is it too ugly to see the old man as a Christ figure? Perhaps ugly, but quite probable. Not only does he "love mankind," but, like the Fisher King, he is sick, unvital, and literally, because of his sickness, sterile. This identification of both Miss Lonelyhearts and the old man as a Christ figure is suggested closely by a parallel identification in the Gawain legend: "In the final development of the story the *Pathos* is shared alike by the representative of the Vegetation Spirit, and the Healer. . . ."[19] The pathos of this identification of the two will be dealt with later from a psychoanalytic perspective, for it is operative upon that level as well. The brilliance of West's achievement, as has been suggested elsewhere, lies not only in the subtle working out of the Grail parallels, but in the working out of other meanings at the same time. It is the Kafkaesque ability to create layers of meaning.

It may be straining to suggest that the horseplay substitutes for the presence of the horse, and perhaps straining to see the cane as a phallus, but not necessarily; for as an accessory of the old man which he is ready to use, the cane is a nice symbolic substitute for the phallus he is unwilling to use. It is impossible, however, to dismiss the prominence rightly given the frog, for it has great symbolic importance, not only in underlining the Grail parallels but in other ways. It is important to note that already, at the end of the fifth chapter, the failure of the quest is suggested: the old man is not rejuvenated. Moreover, the element of perversion dramatizes the enormity of the blight that afflicts the land.

Such pessimistic foreshadowing gains intensity when one realizes that immediately preceding this scene, West has presented a hopeful sign: the children "gravely and carefully" dancing, "a simple dance yet formal" (p. 37). West apparently wished to counterpoint youthful hope and innocence with aged despair and perversion. The description of the dance ("square replacing oblong and being replaced by circle") also can be read as a traditional symbolic statement of order and harmony replacing disorder. More importantly, the dance is a remarkable recreation of the ritual sword dance performed by the youthful

Maruts who "were, by nature and origin, closely connected with spirits of fertility of a lower order."[20] Miss Weston describes the dances as "solemn ceremonial," and notes that a variation of the ritual existed in "the belief among Germanic peoples . . . in a troop of Child souls . . . closely connected with the dominant spirit of Vegetation."[21]

It was naturally impossible for West always to establish exact parallels without rending the fabric of his novel. Nor does he seem to have attempted to match the Grail legend episode for episode: perhaps he felt a too blatant parallel would obscure his other intentions; moreover, perhaps like Joyce he merely wished to universalize his material by fixing it in archetypal forms. That he chose the Grail legend seems in part the result of his own preoccupation with the quest motif, in part the result of the religious subject matter of the novel. Perhaps it pleased West's ironic, pessimistic turn to discover that even this most sacred of Christian stories upon examination revealed the inevitable sexual dynamic.

What should be stressed is that even if West does not follow the legend's chronology of events, even if he has modernized those events and modified them under the influence of his peculiar temperament, he has nevertheless used nearly all of them. The conviction that Miss Weston's book was something of an idea book for West just as it had been to a lesser degree earlier, for Eliot, is inescapable. Only such an explanation helps one to understand the subtle transformations West has worked upon variations of the legend, transformations suggested by Miss Weston's analysis.

The most substantial transformation occurs in the chapter "Miss Lonelyhearts and the Lamb," a chapter which parallels the episode of the Perilous Chapel in the Grail romances. A variant of the episode deals with Arthur's squire, Chaus, who is to accompany the King to the chapel. Arthur bids the lad be ready to ride at dawn. The lad falls asleep, and on waking apparently alone, he rides after Arthur. Finding a chapel in the midst of a graveyard, he enters and sees the body of a knight on a bier surrounded by tapers. The remainder of the story has violent sexual overtones suggesting castration anxiety:

> Chaus takes out one of the tapers, and thrusting the golden can-

> dlestick betwixt hose and thigh, remounts and rides back in search of the King. Before he has gone far he meets a man, black, and foul-favored, armed with a large two-edged knife. He asks has he met King Arthur? The man answers, No, but he has met him, Chaus; he is a thief and a traitor; he has stolen the golden candlestick; unless he gives it up he shall pay for it dearly. Chaus refuses, and the man smites him in the side with the knife. With a loud cry the lad awakes, he is lying in the hall at Cardoil, wounded to death, the knife in his side and the golden candlestick still in his hose.[22]

Such a story seems to have no parallel in the novel, and indeed it is scarcely the story that is transformed so much as Miss Weston's analysis:

> *For this is the story of an initiation* (or perhaps it would be more correct to say the test of fitness for an initiation) *carried out on the astral plane, and reacting with fatal results upon the physical.*
>
> We have already seen in the Naassene document that the Mystery ritual comprised a double initiation, the Lower, into the mysteries of generation, *i.e.*, of physical Life; the higher, into the Spiritual Divine Life, where man is made one with God.
>
> . . . the test for the primary initiation, that into the sources of physical life, would probably consist in a contact with the horrors of physical death, and . . . the tradition of the Perilous Chapel . . . was a reminiscence of the test for this lower initiation.[23]

In a note Miss Weston adds: "the actual initiation would probably consist in enlightenment into the meaning of Lance and Cup, in their sexual juxtaposition." She further describes the rites as "semi-Pagan, semi-Christian."

The chapter's parallels with the Chaus story are superficial ones: both are dreams; both deal with youths; a religious atmosphere (altar and chapel) and the taint of death are in both. Such parallels are hardly substantial. However, West's allegiance, as an analysis reveals, seems less to the romances than to Miss Weston's interpretation.

After an all-night college drinking bout, Miss Lonelyhearts and two other boys buy a lamb to barbecue in the woods. First, however, they intend to sacrifice it to God. Traditionally, sacrifice has been a ritual form of penance or purification or an attempted initiation "into the Spiritual Divine Life, where man is made one with God." This sacrifice has more than spiritual overtones, for the lamb, "a little, stiff-legged thing," and the sacrifice are described in language suggesting virgin rape. After picking "daisies and buttercups" (the semipagan element), the boys proceed with the business at hand:

> When they had worked themselves into a frenzy, he [Miss Lonelyhearts] brought the knife down hard. The blow was inaccurate and made a flesh wound. He raised the knife again and this time the lamb's violent struggles made him miss altogether. (p. 23)

If Freud has not, Miss Weston has made it clear that the lance and cup are sex symbols representing male and female, respectively. It is difficult to conceive of a scene which could have fulfilled the varied criteria of Miss Weston's initiation as well as this one does, for this "initiation carried out on the astral plane" (or its equivalent—a dream) reacts upon, or at least mirrors, a "fatal" flaw (Miss Lonelyhearts' sexual anxieties and disturbance) upon the physical. Moreover, West has not violated the novel's beautifully balanced symbolic structure: the scene carries equally well its narrative, religious, and psychoanalytic weight. Meaning on one level is not sacrificed for meaning on another level.

There are other examples of West's employment of the legend or of Miss Weston's theses, such as the use of fishing imagery to describe Miss Lonelyhearts' religious experience. (This employment of fishing imagery is not an isolated, final occurrence; fishing imagery abounds in the novel.) With respect to such imagery, Miss Weston notes:

> We can affirm with certainty that the Fish is a Life symbol of immemorial antiquity, and that the title of Fisher has, from the earliest ages, been associated with Deities who were held to be specially connected with the origin and preservation of Life.[24]

In *Miss Lonelyhearts,* West has seized upon a myth, just as Joyce and Eliot had in *Ulysses* and *The Waste Land,* in an attempt to bring order to a disordered world, and to give the action a timeless truth. In the legend of the dead Fisher King he found a myth which was rather perfectly suited to his heightened sensitivity to despair and decay.

Although dealing with legend or myth, West does not allow himself to be restricted by it. *Miss Lonelyhearts* is the symbolist masterpiece that it is precisely because West has merely incorporated the Grail and Oedipal legends into a larger conception. More than a modernization of a legend, *Miss Lonelyhearts* is a modern myth.

The myth was ironically conceived; any other conception was probably impossible in a scientific world where the inherited, enduring universe of symbols has collapsed. Dream-bounded societies "within a mythologically charged horizon . . . no longer exist."[25] West's sensibility—a strange blend of irony and faintly mystic intensity—was perhaps a necessary one for the modern mythmaker. Moreover, "humor [being] the touchstone of the truly mythological as distinct from the more literal-minded and sentimental theological mood,"[26] West, as evidenced by the novel, was at home in the mythic mode.

In his study of the archetypal hero, Joseph Campbell defines a composite adventure of the hero which bears a striking resemblance to Miss Lonelyhearts' experience:

> . . . the *separation* or *departure*: . . . (1) "The Call to Adventure," or the signs of the vocation of the hero; (2) "Refusal of the Call," or the folly of the flight from the god; (3) "Supernatural Aid," the unsuspected assistance that comes to one who has undertaken his proper adventure; (4) "The Crossing of the First Threshold"; and (5) "The Belly of the Whale," or the passage into the realm of night. The stage of *the trials and victories of initiation*: . . . (1) "The Road of Trials," or the dangerous aspect of the gods; (2) "The Meeting with the Goddess" (*Magna Mater*), or the bliss of infancy regained; (3) "Woman as the Temptress," the realization and agony of Oedipus; (4) "Atonement with the Father"; (5) "Apotheosis"; and (6) "The Ultimate Boon."[27]

In warning against overly literal readings, Mr. Campbell notes that "the changes rung on the simple scale of the monomyth defy description."[28] The warning notwithstanding, with the exception of a slight modification of order, the composite monomyth describes *Miss Lonelyhearts* so strikingly as scarcely to need comment: The "Call" is the Miss Lonelyhearts job which leads to a priestlike vocation; his fear of hysteria, the "snake," is his "Refusal"; and his ultimate capitulation to God reveals the "folly of his flight." The symbolic "Supernatural Aid," according to Campbell, is often provided by "a little old crone or old man"; and in *Miss Lonelyhearts* the "clean old man," who is associated with a frog (a symbol for the unconscious), provides the hero with an unconscious insight into himself which hastens his "Atonement with the Father." "Crossing the First Threshold" occurs in the chapter "Miss Lonelyhearts and the Dead Pan." Campbell notes: "The Arcadian god Pan is the best known Classical example of this dangerous presence dwelling just beyond the protected zone of the village boundary."[29] And Miss Lonelyhearts' growing catatonia is described in sea imagery clearly suggesting the "night journey" or the descent into the "belly of the whale." Campbell notes, significantly, that the passage of the mythological hero is fundamentally inward.[30]

Miss Lonelyhearts' *trials* or "initiations"—they can hardly be called *victories* in the novel—begin with the dream sacrifice of the lamb. The beginning of his night journey, it has obvious parallels with the following description by Campbell of "The Road of Trials":

> And so it happens that if anyone . . . undertakes for himself the perilous journey into the darkness by descending, either intentionally or unintentionally, into the crooked lanes of his own spiritual labyrinth, he soon finds himself in a landscape of symbolical figures (any one of which may swallow him).[31]

The meaning of West's description of Chapter Three—"the need for taking symbols literally is described through a dream in which a symbol is actually flashed"[32]—begins to become clear. Campbell then adds a remark that not only explains West's meaning but also becomes of great importance when discussing the dream sacrifice of the lamb from a psychoanalytical viewpoint: "The specific psychological difficulties of the dreamer frequently are revealed with touching simplicity and force."[33]

The pastoral interlude with Betty, who is an obvious surrogate for the *Magna Mater,* conveys the "bliss of infancy regained"; that it is a false or, at best, temporary bliss does not thereby invalidate this element of the monomyth. The next characteristic, his encounter with "Woman as Temptress"—Fay Doyle's seduction—induces in him an "Oedipus-Hamlet revulsion." Campbell, in his discussion of "Woman as the Temptress," notes that when this "revulsion remains to beset the soul . . . the world, the body, and woman above all, become the symbols no longer of victory but of defeat."[34] In the novel, after the seduction, is the following passage:

> Soon after Mrs. Doyle left, Miss Lonelyhearts became physically sick . . . his imagination began to work.
>
> He found himself in the window of a pawnshop full of fur coats, diamond rings, watches, shotguns, fishing tackle, mandolins. All these things were the paraphernalia of suffering. . . .
>
> He sat in the window thinking. Man has a tropism for order. Keys in one pocket, change in another. Mandolins are tuned G D A E. The physical world has a tropism for disorder, entropy. Man against nature . . . the battle of the centuries. Keys yearn to mix with change. Mandolins strive to get out of tune. Every order has within it the germ of destruction. All order is doomed. . . . (pp. 73-74)

Finally, Campbell's description of "The Atonement with the Father" is a comment on Miss Lonelyhearts' religious conversion as well:

> The problem of the hero going to meet the father is to open his soul beyond terror to such a degree that he will be ripe to understand how the sickening and insane tragedies of this vast and ruthless cosmos are completely validated in the majesty of Being. The hero transcends life with its peculiar blind spot and for a moment rises to a glimpse of the source. He beholds the face of the father, understands—and the two are atoned.[35]

Ultimately, what is so remarkable about the novel is the range and depth of its archetypal conception. Apparently casual responses are far from casual. The richness of the novel resides in symbolic or archetypal dimension residing in almost every detail. Note, for example, how Campbell's description of the hero who refuses the summons describes Miss Lonelyhearts' responses: "Walled in boredom, hard work, or 'culture,' the subject loses the power of significant affirmative action and becomes a victim to be saved. His flowering world becomes a wasteland of dry stones and his life feels meaningless."[36]

Miss Lonelyhearts is the near perfect work it is because as a myth, it is not a dream—not even a grotesque nightmare. Its pattern, like that of myth, is consciously controlled. Intended to "serve as a powerful picture language for the communication of traditional wisdom," myths "are not only symptoms of the unconscious . . . but also controlled and intended statements of certain spiritual principles."[37] That West consciously constructed his myth to give "certain spiritual principles" a bitter, ironic twist is not only characteristic, but revealing; it suggests that West, like many moderns, was prone to a psychological interpretation of myth. Since Freud's Oedipal studies and Jung's analysis of the collective unconscious, such psychological interpretation has become widespread. West's success in adding this psychoanalytic dimension to the classic archetypal drama of *Miss Lonelyhearts*, in psychoanalyzing Miss Lonelyhearts *imagistically*, is his most briliant achievement, and so subtle an accomplishment that his method is worth some discussion.

West revealed the heart of his psychological method in "Some Notes on Miss L.":

> Psychology has nothing to do with reality nor should it be used as a motivation. The novelist is no longer a psychologist. Psychology can now become something much more important. The great body of case histories can be used in the way the ancient writers used their myths. Freud is your Bullfinch; you can not learn from him.[38]

Freud (psychoanalysis) has delved so deeply into the human psyche that the analytic novel has been rendered sterile. "The novelist is no longer a psychologist," because the novelist can offer no new psychological insights. Instead, "psychology can now become something much more important." "The great body of case histories" can now be used in an archetypal sense. They have already taken on the elements of legend and should be so used. West's assertion that Miss Lonelyhearts' "case is classical" was not mere legpull, for West has taken a "classical case history" —an Oedipus complex—and, by the use of brilliant imagery, translated it into a work of art.

Miss Lonelyhearts' Oedipal homosexuality, which is developed ironically, was suggested by West when he explained that "Miss Lonelyhearts became the portrait of a priest of our time who has a religious experience" *with Freud* "in mind." While such a comment need not make one suspicious of "the portrait," the imagery—which West makes emphatically clear is his—and various episodes should, for all of them point to an Oedipal homosexuality.

West apparently desired the reader to approach the novel with a Freudian orientation, for the allusiveness of his method suggests that he relied upon his readers' recognition of the complex and knowledge of Freud, just as Sophocles had counted on his audience's familiarity with the Oedipus story. Only by doing so could they have suppressed superfluities and achieved compression of such enormous power. Thus, nowhere in *Miss Lonelyhearts* does West take time to suggest through commentary that Miss Lonelyhearts has a homosexual Oedipal complex. He doesn't have to, because the reader unconsciously responds to key images. Ultimately, as a result of the train of suggestions set in motion by a few suggestive images, the entire emotional-intellectual complex falls into place with the swiftness of an axe falling.

Even upon a first reading, one is struck by the number of phallic images in *Miss Lonelyhearts*. Individually they are unimpressive, but, as always in West, their cumulative number and effect is overpowering. More important, the images occur during moments of emotional disturbance. On one bad day, "the point of the pencil broke, the handle of the razor fell off." (p. 25) Later, after *l'affaire* Fay Doyle,

> A tortured high light twisted on the blade of a gift knife, a battered horn grunted with pain.
>
> . . . . .
>
> A trumpet, marked to sell for $2.49, gave the call to battle and Miss Lonelyhearts plunged into the fray. First he formed a phallus of old watches and rubber boots. . . . (pp. 73-74)

These images gain in suggestive power because of the rapidity with which West suggests Miss Lonelyhearts' disturbance. West casts the first innuendo eight pages after the novel begins. Shrike, praising the "intelligence" of Miss Farkis, "by carving two enormous breasts in the air with his hands" (pp. 12-13), finds Miss Lonelyhearts annoyed and remarks: " 'Oh, so you don't care for women, eh?' " (p. 13) However, because the conversation rapidly shifts to Christ, one hardly notices Shrike's hint.

Soon after, in a scene with Betty, Miss Lonelyhearts' sexual maladjustment is dramatically introduced. He reaches inside her clothes and fondles her naked breast, simply because he is "unable to think of anything else to do" (p. 29).

Later, the violence with which he attacks the "clean old man" with a fluting voice who "went soft in their [Miss Lonelyhearts' and Gates'] arms and started to giggle" (p. 39) makes one further question the normality of his response. Twisting the arm of the old man, he felt that "he was twisting the arm of all the sick and miserable, broken and betrayed, inarticulate and impotent. He was twisting the arms of Desperate, Broken-hearted, Sick-of-it-all, Disillusioned-with-tubercular-husband" (p. 42). There is a strong implication that in revenging himself on this homosexual, he is in reality identifying with him, and therefore wreaking vengeance upon himself. Sadism and masochism have become fused.

The violence is precipitated because the "clean old man" reminds Miss Lonelyhearts of a frog he once accidentally stepped upon. In beholding the old man (who calls up the frog), Miss Lonelyhearts is penetrating into the labyrinth of his unconscious. The old man is an objectification of Miss Lonelyhearts' unconscious desires, of his repressed homosexuality. The violence of Miss Lonelyhearts' response has its origin in the massiveness of the threat posed to his conscious. That Miss Lonelyhearts' repression is significantly weakened by this episode is suggested by an incident in a park which occurs but two pages later. Slumping "down on a bench," Miss Lonelyhearts watches a Mexican War obelisk begin to behave dangerously like a gigantic erection:

> The stone shaft cast a long, rigid shadow on the walk in front of him. He sat staring at it without knowing why until he noticed that it was lengthening in rapid jerks, not as shadows usually lengthen. He grew frightened and looked up quickly at the monument. It seemed red and swollen in the dying sun, as though it were about to spout a load of granite seed. (pp. 44-45)

The most impressive of the phallic images, like the others it is presented with the same casualness with which West conveys Miss Lonelyhearts' preoccupation with women's breasts.

West reinforces the images which suggest an Oedipal homosexuality by numerous allusions to Miss Lonelyhearts' sexual unresponsiveness and revulsion. Generally, West presents the allusion in the form of an image. Here Miss Lonelyhearts is contemplating Fay Doyle's letter:

> Against the dark mahogany desk top, the cheap paper took on rich flesh tones. He thought of Mrs. Doyle as a tent, hair-covered and veined, and of himself as the skeleton in a water closet. . . . When he made the skeleton enter the flesh tent, it flowered at every joint.
>
> But despite these thoughts, he remained as dry and cold as a polished bone. . . . (pp. 62-63)

Sometimes West is more direct in his description of Miss Lonelyhearts' unusual sexual responses:

> He tried to excite himself into eagerness by thinking of the play Mary made with her breasts. . . . But the excitement refused to come. If anything, he felt colder than before he had started to think of women. *It was not his line.* (p. 46. Emphasis mine.)

West has pointed out "the element of self-torture by conscious sinning" in the episode with Mary Shrike; this becomes so much the greater when one realizes his natural distaste for the type of sinning in which he is indulging. Yet, as if this almost explicit statement of Miss Lonelyhearts' abnormality is not enough, West continues to reinforce it. When Fay Doyle seduces him, Miss Lonelyhearts notes that "he had always been the pursuer, but now found a strange pleasure in having the roles reversed. He drew back when she reached for a kiss"; and again, a few lines later, "he pulled away with a rude jerk" (p. 66). Soon after Fay Doyle leaves, he becomes ill. Finally, when he meets the cripple, Peter Doyle, and reads his letter, the following telling act occurs:

> While Miss Lonelyhearts was puzzling out the crabbed writing, Doyle's damp hand accidentally touched his under the table. He jerked away, but then drove his hand back and forced it to clasp the cripple's. After finishing the letter, he did not let go, but pressed it firmly with all the love he could manage. At first the

> cripple covered his embarrassment by disguising the meaning of the clasp with a handshake, but he soon gave in to it and they sat silently, hand in hand. (p. 113)

All of these images and episodes are suggestive, but to complete the picture of Miss Lonelyhearts' complex, one must turn to an interpretation of his dreams. Following good psychoanalytic technique, West not only exploits dream analysis, he demands that his reader practice it. Miss Lonelyhearts' first dream occurs in "Miss Lonelyhearts and the Lamb," the chapter with the most violent sexual overtones. What is the result of this dream where lamb = purity and knife = phallus? The following castration anxiety: "The knife broke on the altar."[39]

Following three pages after the association of a phallic symbol, a snake, with the "name of Christ," this further association of the "lamb" with castration suggests the sexual origin of Miss Lonelyhearts' religious conversion. This hint becomes more than a suggestion when Miss Lonelyhearts begins to retreat into his rocklike catatonia.[40] In a dream bordering on hallucination, West crystallizes Miss Lonelyhearts' suppressed homosexuality in a sharp image of anal penetration: "Later a train rolled into a station where he was a reclining statue holding a clock. . . ." (p. 124)

Finally, the very image used to describe Miss Lonelyhearts' religious conversion is highly sexual and ironic. Upon perceiving that his room "was full of grace," "he felt clean and fresh. His heart was a rose and in his skull another rose bloomed." Later, he felt a grace as "clean as the innersides of the inner petals of a newly forced rosebud" (p. 140). Though the rose may symbolize "Paradise, grace, and Divine Love,"[41] in the general sexual context of the novel, to read a traditional rather than a Freudian meaning into it is to miss the novel's ultimate irony. The conversion is the natural culmination of Miss Lonelyhearts' homosexual castration complex. In his schizophrenic state, Miss Lonelyhearts' repressed castration complex emerges in a symbolic identification of himself with the rose—the female sexual organs.[42] What Miss Lonelyhearts really accepts is his castration. The religious conversion is really a conversion from latent to overt homosexuality; so is the ending. The final embrace between Miss Lonelyhearts and Doyle is, as Stanley Edgar Hyman has noted, "a homosexual tableau—the men locked in embrace while the woman stands helplessly by."[43] Hyman has also noted that "it is West's ultimate irony that the symbolic embrace they manage at the end is one penetrating the body of the other with a bullet."[44]

Alan Ross has remarked that "*Balso Snell* analyses . . . the disintegration of the Self, and its illusion of superiority at its most pathetic moment of neurotic isolation";[45] the remark as aptly describes *Miss Lonelyhearts.* Perhaps the overwhelming sense of compassion one feels for Miss Lonelyhearts results from the sincere pathos with which West conveys Miss Lonelyhearts' neurotic isolation; similarly, the tinge of indignation one feels may result from the merciless manner in which West pursues, undermines, and destroys him. West's ironic treatment of Miss Lonelyhearts is not, however, a question of mercy or its lack. Perhaps the added ironic fillip did please West's mordant pessimism; and perhaps it did not. Whatever the reason, it seems clear that the ugliness of this homosexual turn illuminates an important aspect of West's peculiar sensibility—his response to suffering.

Just before Miss Lonelyhearts twists the arm of the "clean old man," West attempts to explain in his usual psychological shorthand why Miss Lonelyhearts does so:

> Miss Lonelyhearts felt as he had felt years before, when he had accidentally stepped on a small frog. Its spilled guts had filled him with pity, but when its suffering had become real to his senses, his pity had turned to rage and he had beaten it frantically until it was dead. (p. 41)

That frog seems to offer a clue to West's unconscious as well, for James F. Light suggests that West had much the same response to suffering:

> The gusto with which West described the sordidness and suffering of the people in the hotel, the fascination which he found in portraying the hotel guests as inhuman clowns and grotesques, the way in which he reveled in the very details he deplored—all these, perhaps, formed some private masochistic alchemy by which West tried to erase the vision of suffering humanity he saw around him.[46]

Only such a remark—which has the force of a discovery—

can explain the strange tonal quality of West's novels; only such a remark can explain why West should have added a powerful latent homosexuality to Miss Lonelyhearts' other problems. Miss Lonelyhearts is, in some respects, West's suffering frog.[47]

Miss Lonelyhearts may strike many, particularly religious readers, as an unpleasant, even ugly novel, and not without some justification. Nevertheless, despite its many unfortunate anti-religious overtones, one misunderstands West and does him a disservice if one fails to realize that the attack is against that kind of religiosity which seeks to escape involvement in human suffering by explaining and justifying its existence. If *Miss Lonelyhearts* upsets its readers, it is because in various forms it reveals the cancerous deceits by which men disguise their indifference, by which they escape involvement in, as W. H. Auden put it, the "human position" of suffering. *Miss Lonelyhearts* is a moving, powerful novel because it is the comic, pathetic, and perhaps even tragic story of a holy fool, who as quester is ultimately made scapegoat by his inability to fathom the mystery of human suffering or to forget it.

Still the novel, another example of West's "particular kind of joking," is much more. The subtle symbols, the allusive conception, and the bitter ironies are all part of West's attempt to disguise his emotional involvement in an agonizing perception, and are his way of preventing the novel from being sentimental. They make a simple reading impossible. *Miss Lonelyhearts* is an enormously compressed and complex novel; to pretend that it is simple is to pretend that West was neither a symbolist nor a highly allusive writer.

Perhaps the novel's conception precludes a widely agreed-upon interpretation; even now West's sensibility as reflected in the novel is beyond the purview of most of his readers. However, with effort, and with an awareness of what is being done in post-World War II European and American fiction and drama, they can now begin to read rather than misread the novel.

Miss Lonelyhearts is not any one of the interpretations presented in this chapter—it is all of them. The layers of meaning in the novel do not, as they might seem to, sit on top of one another as oil sits on water; they dissolve into each other. More than a mechanical sum of its parts, the novel is a *Gestalt* and must be seen as one. A symbolist prose poem, it is neither as moving and religious as its simple narrative suggests; as grand, heroic, and affirmative as its mythic conception indicates; nor as thoroughly savage, cynical, and obscene as its psychological dimension leads one to believe. The purity of each line has been blurred by the others.

In its poignant evocation of religious atrophy, its ironic antiheroism, and its pervasive and faintly sickening psychological reduction of human behavior, *Miss Lonelyhearts* is a summation of our time. It is an affirmation of despair and a protest—a raging, mythic, mocking, agonizing protest against a world so flattened and absurd that true compassion is unendurable.

VI. A Cool Million

Turning to *A Cool Million* after reading *Miss Lonelyhearts* is like examining a paste jewel after one has beheld a diamond. As a work of art it is hardly worthy of sustained comment. It is a bag of tricks, some of which are brilliantly effective, and it fails to achieve anything beyond a few laughs. The point of the novel —a penetrating one—dissipates itself in slapstick; and the style—clever as it sometimes is—is an unfortunate departure from West's usual manner. To compare it with the style of *Miss Lonelyhearts* is painful. This is as true of plot as of style, for the plot, while amusing, is a facile one; and though many of the incidents are strikingly ingenious, they do little more than reflect West's extravagant fancy.

For all this, the novel is a difficult one to analyze—not because it is a difficult work, but because there is a chasm between serious content and facetious expression which can only be deepened by discussion. As a result, there is a danger that a detailed analysis will not capture the tone of the novel. The problem is irritating, but a difficult one to avoid.

The first and, in many respects, the only things that strike the reader's eye are the style and the incidents. The style is noticeable in a way one wishes that it was not; the incidents are another matter. They fall so swiftly upon each other that one feels he is watching a melodramatic, speeded-up, silent film serial on the order of *The Perils of Pauline*. Lemuel Pitkin, a Horatio Alger in reverse, never escapes from his escapades unscathed. On the contrary, all the isolated and complexly interwoven episodes lead to disaster. A throwback to the sly leer and boisterous ridicule of *Balso Snell*, *A Cool Million* is similarly structured—or similarly formless; only this picaresque journey traces the stages of Lemuel's frantic dismantling, relieved by occasional glimpses of "frail" Betty Prail. Within a short time after beginning the novel, one is not asking, "What will this all-American boy and girl escape from next?" but, "What won't they escape from next?" The incidents are, on the whole, satirically well chosen; and some of them are genuinely funny. It is difficult, however, to escape the feeling that all these comic incidents merely prove that West had a great deal of talent and that he wasted it in writing *A Cool Million.*

The style still has glimmerings of the old West that further convince the reader of waste. Now and then, there are flashes of fine writing:

> Mr. Jefferson mounted a box to introduce Mr. Whipple.
> "Fellow townsmen, Southerners, Protestants, Americans," he began. "You have been called here to listen to the words of Shagpoke Whipple, one of the few Yanks whom we of the South can trust and respect. He ain't no nigger-lover, he don't give a damn for Jewish culture, and he knows the fine Italian hand of the Pope when he sees it. Mr. Whipple . . ."[1]

But there is altogether too much wooden prose:

> His position permitted him a great deal of leisure. He used his spare time to good advantage by visiting the many interesting spots for which New York City is justly famous. (p. 197)
>
> . . . . .
>
> At first Lem had some difficulty in using the wooden leg with which the hospital authorities had equipped him. Practice, however, makes perfect . . .
> It goes without saying that the two friends were not satisfied to remain hostlers. . . . (p. 235)

For all the affected gaiety, it is dull; and it is so despite West's economy. In this novel, the economy that was used so effectively in *Miss Lonelyhearts* serves no artistic purpose. West merely uses it to crowd—with great speed and agility—more clever incidents into his short novel. There is nothing praiseworthy, per se, in this. Nor is the mock-heroic, as West uses it, the most difficult of styles: cleverness and a fine ear are all that are necessary, and West has already proven that he possessed these.

If West's use of the mock-heroic were consistently witty, it would not be so offensive; but so much of it is of the cheapest sort. Often it merely consists of discovering an excruciatingly weak word or phrase and incorporating it into the sentence: "On the floor was a silk rug that must have cost more than a thousand dollars" (p. 168); "This terrible intelligence made our hero literally groan with anguish" (p. 173); or "he was a pretty fair boxer . . ." (p. 154). However, even this device is clever when one considers how much of the mock-heroic style consists of stock-in-trade melodramatic vocabulary: "Our hero," "poor lad," "youth," and "strong, spirited lad."

Nor do the author's intrusions enhance the work. Generally, they merely allow West to tie together the loose strands of his narrative: "It might interest the reader to know that I was right in my surmise. An interior decorator, on passing the house, had been greatly struck by its appearance" (p. 145); or, to get on with his narrative: "It is with reluctance, that I leave Miss Prail in the lecherous embrace of Tom Baxter to begin a new chapter . . ." (p. 155).

West's use of irony—evident in the "reluctance" with which he leaves Miss Prail—is somewhat better but really does little to redeem the work. Most painful of all, however, is the extent to which the melodramatic, mock-heroic style forced West to discard his greatest asset—his figurative language, which in this novel is so rare as to be nonexistent. The poetry is gone; and when figures do occur—the following is typical—they are but shells of the ones in *Miss Lonelyhearts*: "With all the formality of a priest, Shagpoke turned to our hero and laid his hand on his shoulder" (p. 186).

West is much better when he is able to create a scene, when he satirizes a stock character or a traditional story. Thus the speech by Israel Satinpenny and the event that follows allow West to add real, if humorous, social criticism. At the same time that West, through Israel, rejects Rousseau (I'm no Rousseauistic philosopher. I know you can't put the clock back."), he pays his respects to the two prophets of decline who influenced him: "The day of vengeance is here. The star of the paleface is sinking and he knows it. Spengler has said so; Valery has said so" (p. 233).

Somewhat different from such incidents, which allow West to

bring into play his ear for dialogue and his eye for amusing detail, is the fashion in which West subtly modifies the Cinderella story. Betty Prail, "our Cinderella," while in the "clutches" of the Slemp family is thus not only persecuted by the women of the house, but also beaten by Lawyer Slemp, "a deacon in the Church and a very stern man." The leering sexual innuendo in West's tale tears away another mask of propriety, and the sordid reality—the power of sex—is once again revealed:

> Mr. Slemp beat Betty regularly and enthusiastically. He had started these beatings when she first came from the asylum as a little girl, and did not stop them when she became a splendid woman. He beat her twice a week on her bare behind with his bare hand.
>
> . . . although he was exceedingly penurious, [he] always gave her a quarter when he had finished beating her. (p. 156)

The success of the passage results from its sly undertones: e.g., "twice a week" suggests the rhythm of Deacon Slemp's sexual appetite. When West brings into play this ability to seize upon suggestive detail, the writing is almost fine.

Thus, the passages describing the girls' rooms in Wu Fong's establishment are a genuine delight. A passage from this section of the novel reveals as well the offhand manner in which West presents much of his social criticism:

> The depression hit Wu Fong as hard as it did more respectable merchants . . . when the Hearst papers began their "Buy America" campaign he decided to get rid of all the foreigners in his employ and turn his establishment into an hundred per centum American place.
>
> Although in 1928 it would have been exceedingly difficult for him to have obtained the necessary girls, by 1934 things were different. . . .
>
> He engaged Mr. Asa Goldstein to redecorate the house. . . . In general the results were as follows:
>
> Lena Haubengrauber from Perkiomen Creek, Bucks County, Pennsylvania. Her rooms were filled with painted pine furniture and decorated with slip ware, spatter ware, chalk ware and "Gaudy Dutch." Her simple farm dress was fashioned of bright gingham.
>
> . . . . .

> Mary Judkins from Jugtown Hill, Arkansas. Her walls were lined with oak puncheons chinked with mud. Her mattress was stuffed with field corn and covered by a buffalo rope. There was real dirt on her floors. She dressed in homespun, butternut stained, and wore a pair of men's boots.
>
> . . . . .
>
> Princess Roan Fawn from Two Forks, Oklahoma Indian Reservation, Oklahoma. Her walls were papered with birch bark to make it look like a wigwam and she did business on the floor. Except for a necklace of wolf's teeth, she was naked under her bull's-eye blanket. (pp. 202-04)

Such writing, though still but a shadow of West's best, is all too rare in *A Cool Million.* Such passages are showpieces and not part of the wares the novel is selling. Only occasionally, here and in a bit of dialogue where West's fine ear plays a part, does one find a fragment stamped with West's usual mark, "Made by West":

> Shagpoke mounted the box which Mr. Jefferson vacated and waited for the cheering to subside. He began by placing his hand on his heart. "I love the South," he announced. "I love her because her women are beautiful and chaste, her men brave and gallant, and her fields warm and fruitful. . . ." (p. 254)

West's heavyhandedness is deliberate; by drawing attention to itself, the rhetoric helps to expose the deception underneath. West always used rhetoric to reveal or expose fraud. To a large extent, it supplies the strident quality in his writing. Prevalent as Shrike or Whipple's rhetoric is, it is not subtle. However, a man "yelling fire" and "indicating where some of the smoke is coming from" is not seeking subtlety. To look for this kind of subtlety in West is to misunderstand him and the fact that the strength of his rhetoric resides in the finger it points at the tyrant and the tormentor, at the delusion and the danger. Moreover, despite or perhaps because of its strident quality, it imparts a certain comic warmth to the novels which they otherwise would lack. Certainly when this rhetoric does not appear (it is lacking, for example, in *The Day of the Locust*), there is a resultant coolness.

A Cool Million is surely warmly comic; but beneath its comic surface there is a sinister social and political analysis. Written in

1934, in the fully-felt horror of the depression, the slapstick, as usual in West, disguises a tortured humanistic protest—in this instance, a protest against depression America. As such, the drama of the National Revolutionary Party's rise to power is a warning as well as a mirror of the society. As always in West, the mirror is a carnival mirror—distorting much, but in the main exaggerating and emphasizing the reality before it.

Again, West is commenting upon "eternal verities"—this time peculiar American social and political truths. The epigraph, "John D. Rockefeller would give a cool million to have a stomach like yours," is extremely suggestive. An "old saying," it suggests an entire state of mind composed of idealism, frustration, resentment, and compensation. More than anything, however, it is an irrelevant bromide. This observation should establish one's attitude before he takes up the novel, for the novel is riddled with bromides and empty platitudes. They are Marie Antoinette's "cake" for the masses; and West is intensely concerned with this "cake." Thus, Alan Ross' remark that "in the course of the book almost every popular American bogy is caricatured,"[2] while accurate, neglects to make clear the other side of the coin: that West is as concerned with unmasking an illusory ideal as with an illusory fear. The following passage shows but one of the Hydra's heads:

> "Capital is international; its home is in London and in Amsterdam. Labor is international; its home is in Moscow.
>
> . . . . .
>
> "We must drive the Jewish international bankers out of Wall Street! We must destroy the Bolshevik labor unions! We must purge our country of all the alien elements and ideas that now infest her!" (p. 188)

The other head is found in such comments as " 'This is the land of opportunity . . .' " (p. 149); and " 'By honesty and industry, you cannot fail to succeed' " (p. 150). The two, the bogy and the bromide, are wonderfully fused in the following typical remark:

> "Rank socialism was and is rampant. How could I, Shagpoke Whipple, ever bring myself to accept a program which promised to take from American citizens their inalienable birthright; the right to sell their labor and their children's labor without restrictions as to either price or hours?" (p. 186)

In such passages, West is creating a society wherein illusions are "rampant," and by playing off illusions against reality, he attacks the cherished illusion of Americanism, or "The American Way of Life." *A Cool Million* is an attempt to dramatize the artificiality and dangers inherent in such an ideal, for, in West, ideals that have their foundation in fiction are sources of frustration.

Behind the slapstick there is an exhaustive attempt to reveal, in linear and inevitable fashion, the idealistic but dangerous paradoxes inherent in Americanism. West proceeds by confronting the ideal with the realities of depression America. The novel follows two diverging lines—one ascending, the other descending. Shagpoke Whipple, untouched by reality, follows his illusions to their ultimate conclusion; Lemuel Pitkin, on the other hand, "touched" by reality, follows his fate to its logical conclusion—destruction.

West is here treating the problem of success and failure in American society and trying to show that the successful betray the society and the society betrays the failure. The irony is all the more painful when one realizes that cherished illusions remain untouched. Wests hammers again and again at this central theme: when reality does not accord with the premises of American society, it is the reality which is re-viewed in a new light, not the premise. This is the significance of Whipple's final masterpiece of rhetoric to his followers. Reality destroys everything—but illusions. West's pessimism in *A Cool Million* is as deep as ever. In West, all may change but this dark world view, this concern with reality and illusions—the tonal and thematic threads that unite all his work.

It would be an error to believe that West's analysis was pertinent to the depression thirties but not to the present. The depression was a catalyst and therefore speeded the process of recognition; the paradoxes inherent in the American system, however, have always been there. The depression merely dramatized the paradoxes—the disease—by increasing the fever; the fever, however, is not the disease.

The disease, West would have his readers believe, is something much more subtle; and when West has Whipple utter the following remark, he has struck the dominant chord of the work. It is the springboard from which to view the entire novel, for it contains the tired illusory clichés, the demogoguery, and the ambiguity which characterize the novel.

> "America," he said with great seriousness, "is the land of

> opportunity. . . . This is not a matter of opinion, it is one of faith. On the day that Americans stop believing it, on that day will America be lost." (p. 150)

Before one can fully appreciate this and similar comments, one must understand how West has modified his use of the cliché in *A Cool Million.*

In *Balso Snell,* West's clichés were essentially stylistic—that is, literary; they had little relevance, with but few exceptions, to attitudes and beliefs. In *Miss Lonelyhearts,* there is a change. Man's deepest feelings about life have been engaged; but they are made puerile by clichéd expression. They have been made so because West wanted his readers to feel the fundamental inadequacy of these expressions. Products of a desperate search, their validity is doubted by Miss Lonelyhearts and scorned by Shrike. They are answers or, more accurately, attempts at answers that never quite come off or satisfy. As a result, one turns away from the clichés in *Miss Lonelyhearts* in distaste, or with a feeling that West, through trickery, has artfully but perhaps artificially destroyed their validity.

Though one may come away from the clichés in *A Cool Million* with similar feelings, he must recognize that its clichés are of a different order. They are not solutions, but premises; and as premises, they allow West to analyze their validity dramatically and, he hopes, to unmask their unreality. Such "unmasking" was not possible in *Miss Lonelyhearts,* but it is possible in *A Cool Million;* and West pursues this task with a vicious sense of dedication. The "dismantling of Lemuel Pitkin" is, in a vital sense, the "dismantling" of clichéd illusions. Clichéd premise after premise is put forth, examined, satirized, confronted with reality, and then scathingly rejected. West, however, never rejects a premise directly, nor does he even question it. That is not his way in *A Cool Million.* Realizing that "givens" are not susceptible to challenge, West prefers to demolish them by demonstrating, through various illuminating incidents, how absurdly divorced from reality they are. He does not debate, he ridicules—a method that is not quite fair but is effective.

The effectiveness of West's ridicule is heightened by an ambiguous tone. By assuming an ingenuous pose, as if he accepted the clichés, West offers the reader no resistance. It is as if he is telling the reader that while he personally agrees with the premise, he, after all, cannot be held responsible for Lem's continued dismantling as a consequence of these premises. West's is a subtle form of Fabian tactic, extremely difficult to counterattack. As if this were not enough, West is using, in most cases, the very words of his audience against them. After all, he seems to be saying, they are *your* clichés.

The amazing thing is that West does not conquer. His failure to do so is one of the major defects of the novel; for if the novel has merit, it is not stylistic, but thematic, and except for the most obvious bogy, one unfortunately almost never notices the theme or, if one does, only in passing. It is not until one's second or third reading that one begins to see the sinister undercurrent beneath the comic surface. Once this has been seen, one discovers that West's analysis, extreme though it is, is neither farfetched nor trivial—certainly not so trivial that the reader should concern himself with a single person in the novel, whether that person be Whipple or Pitkin. Alan Ross' contention that Shagpoke Whipple is "the villain of the story"[3] is too pat. The villain is not Whipple, but what Whipple represents: the blind, uncritical idealism, the simple, uncomplicated world view of society at large. It is with this world view that West is concerned; and it is the central point that he is trying to dramatize about America. It is a point well suited to barbed satire, and West attacks it with comic gusto.

Much of the comedy is created by the inevitable ironies to be found in any situation where illusions persist in the face of brutal attack, but much of it also is due to a stale, unimaginative, lifeless flattening of character, expression, and response. Thus, while West's characters—even in his major works—are never seen in the round, those in *A Cool Million* are not even visible in relief. Not only are they predictable, they are absolutely changeless: Whipple's speech at the end echoes Whipple's speech at the beginning; Lemuel, unlike his namesake Lemuel Gulliver, is not at the end of his "travels" a "carping critic of the society"; and Betty Prail leaves one too speechless to comment. Lack of complication can hardly be carried further.

Not only does West flatten his characters, he flattens their expression—making it as spineless as possible within the limits of acceptable taste, and as empty of implication. In keeping with this flat presentation of speech, it is only fitting and proper that the novel be laced generously with clichés; and, incredibly, there is not a hint of depth or dimension in one of them:

> "By honesty and industry, you cannot fail to succeed." (p. 150)
>
> . . . . .
>
> "My boy, I believe I once told you that you had an almost certain chance to succeed because you were born poor and on a farm. Let me now tell you that your chance is even better because you have been in prison." (p. 173)
>
> . . . . .
>
> "America is still a young country," Mr. Whipple said, assuming his public manner, "and like all young countries, it is rough and unsettled. Here a man is a millionaire one day and a pauper the next, but no one thinks the worse of him. . . ." (p. 174)

Now and then one of West's clichés stuns, not because of its startling originality, but because of an ambiguity which is a function of the reader's own attitude. When the reader hears his own voice most clearly, that is when he sees the greatest ambiguity and feels most uncomfortable; for it is not pleasant to hear one's private thoughts expressed in such banal and extreme fashion. It is as if West has touched on something that, whether true or not, is extremely personal. The reader's laugh is an uneasy one because it is charged with shame.

> Apropos of this, it is lamentable but a fact, nevertheless, that the inferior races greatly desire the women of their superiors. This is why the Negroes rape so many white women in our southern states. (p. 169)
>
> . . . . .
>
> (Wu Fong was a great stickler for detail, and, like many another man, if he had expended as much energy and thought honestly he would have made even more money without having to carry the stigma of being a brothel-keeper. . . .) (p. 170)

These latter clichés differ from the former in not being susceptible to refutation through experience; perhaps for this reason more than any other they are so provocative.

On the whole, however, West is not concerned with this type of cliché except as a tension-provoking device. Though he uses it as part of his attempt to show the inadequacy of stereotyped responses, he is much more concerned with stereotyped responses that are demonstrably inadequate. Time and again West shows the perversion in these responses. Shagpoke Whipple's explanation of why he has been sent to prison is a classic example:

> "It's a long story," said Mr. Whipple with a sigh. "But the long and short of it is that the Rat River National failed and its depositors sent me here."
>
> "Such is the gratitude of the mob, but in a way I can't blame them," Mr. Whipple said with all the horse sense for which he was famous. "Rather do I blame Wall Street and the Jewish international bankers. They loaded me up with a lot of European and South American bonds, then they forced me to the wall. It was Wall Street working hand in hand with the communists that caused my downfall." (p. 172)

It would be an error to suppose that Shagpoke is less than completely sincere; and it is this sincerity that is so terrible, for he is not a hypocrite spouting off cant, but an honest believer. Encountering such a passage, one feels the sinister undertone of the novel. Whipple *is* a sinister character, but when Ross calls him "a believer in American opportunism," he seems to be missing the point; for that is precisely what he is not. Yet, instead of diminishing the danger, his dedication merely increases it. The frightening paradox in his character—and West would have the reader see this character as the personification of as well as spokesman for Americanism—is that he *is* a man of principles. Ironically, however, his principles rarely get in his way. Despite West's clearly intended irony, one does both Whipple and West an injustice to call Whipple a hypocrite. West had something more subtle in mind; he makes a point of showing that Whipple does have a narrow but real humanity (he aids Lem when the latter loses his leg), as well as honesty and integrity:

> "When I left jail, it was my intention to run for office again. But I discovered to my great amazement and utter horror that my party, the Democratic Party, carried not a single plank in its platform that I could honestly endorse. . . ." (p. 186)

The problem of honesty troubles the mind, for West, greatly concerned with paradoxes in this novel, seems to be making the point that honesty, even to a high ideal, is not always praiseworthy. Once again, West is dealing with the problem of illusions *vs.* reality, and stressing that honesty—indeed, any ideal—is meaningless unless rooted in reality and in a recognition of the humanitarian consequences of that fidelity. The notion reflects West's humanitarian bias in its most extreme form.

Whipple's honesty and fidelity to a high ideal—that of delivering America from her enemies and making her again "great"—not only fails to be admirable but is dangerous, precisely because of his incapacity to analyze the consequences of his ideals. They are not only hollow ideals, they are ideals that are insufficiently understood. As a result, Whipple is left, in a significant sense, *without* ideals, for his ideals have no reference to reality.

When Whipple voices the central paradox of the novel, "The American Spirit . . . [is] the spirit of fair play and open competition" (p. 172), he has no real understanding of the implications involved in such a statement. It is natural that he should not, for when this remark is placed beside the following ones to the effect that "the world is an oyster that but waits for hands to open it" (p. 149), that America "is the land of opportunity", that she "takes care of the honest and industrious and never fails them as long as they are both" (p. 150), and that honest and industrious people such as Lem have a "right to expect certain rewards" (p. 254), there evolves a deceptively simple but psychologically complex attitude which, greatly oversimplified, seems to take the following form: America is the land of opportunity. Hence prosperity in America is the natural state of the honest and industrious. Those who are American and prosperous—Rockefeller and Ford—are therefore honest and industrious; those who are not prosperous must of necessity, then, be dishonest or lazy or both, thereby proving that those who merit reward, in the main, receive it. If they do not receive it, it is because someone is not "playing fair" or someone is stifling "open competition." This is true because virtue *is* (and "is," West emphasizes, has become dangerously confused with "should be") rewarded. When it is not, "arch-enemies of the American Spirit: Wall Street and the Communists" (p. 172) must be at fault.

The entire attitude has its foundation in an idealistic emphasis on "freedom." Freedom, however, has a way of becoming confused in Whipple's mind with the notion that "all is permitted." Thus, Whipple is able to escape from an understanding of the fraudulent business ethics shown in the "chamber of American Horrors" by the justification that "the grandmother didn't have to buy the bonds unless she wanted to" (p. 242). True, but irrelevant. His concept of "total freedom" has blinded him. It is this blindness to the paradoxes inherent in his use of "freedom" and "fair play and open competition" that is the essence of his character. His indifference to his confusion allows him to escape the consequences of his ideals and allows him to avoid having his principles get in his way.

Pitkin, however, is less sophisticated. He is unable to juggle the paradoxes and, so unencumbered, weave his way through American life. Unaware that he is on complex field with many obstacles that must be avoided, his faith that the road is straight, simple, and narrow results in his following an unswerving path to destruction. Even when he does make a feeble attempt to escape, he merely jumps aside and continues down the same path. He is unable to realize that the road that he—a "kin" to the "pit"?—follows is strewn with pitfalls. Though he escapes the combined forces of "the international Jewish bankers and the Communists" attacking Shagpoke's "Leather Shirts," he immediately becomes a victim of Elmer Hainey's crooked scheme.

In tracing the career of Lemuel Pitkin, West takes almost every stereotype attributed to the all-American boy, and then savagely proceeds to examine and modify it in order to show that the "virtues" implied in such a person are not virtues, or, if they are, the result of such "virtues" is not a Horatio Alger-like career but a Horatio Alger-like career in reverse. Thus, not only does West unmask the stereotype, he unfolds the inevitable destruction of the "accurately described" American boy, once the veil of illusion has been lifted from his image.

Lem fails because, in reality, as a farm boy he is not an Abe Lincoln but a country bumpkin; because his poverty is not a source of inspiration but of exploitation; because his innocence is not purity but naïveté; because his honesty is not mere honesty but stupidity; and because his trust is nothing more than gullibility. This is Lem as he really is, and yet, incredibly, this is the person who is exalted at the end of the novel. Ironic? It is merely

West's most acid comment about America's vision. So attached to its principles is the society that it is unable to modify them even when they are a violent affront to the facts of life.

West takes pains to exhibit this tendency in American society in comic scene after scene. However, the tendency is too frightening to arouse even a healthy chuckle. The unquestioning allegiance to a closed, air-tight, "illogical" outlook is far too dangerous because it is not susceptible to reason or refutation. The danger is all the greater when one realizes that within the system certain words have assumed hypnotic force. They are almost ritualistic in their suggestive power and, as such, stir emotional, not intellectual, responses.

Thus, when Whipple repeatedly speaks of "communists" and "parisitical international bankers," the labels—and not only these, but "Americanism," "freedom" and "free enterprise" as well—have assumed an inflammatory significance that transcends their original meaning. That West wishes his reader to realize the prevalence and power of these charged words is revealed by their repeated appearance in the novel and by their capacity to incite the crowd to riot. Twice the crowd is aroused by Whipple's jargonistic oratory, and each time its response is a violent one. Five years before *The Day of the Locust,* West has sensed the nature of the anonymous crowd. In the riot in *A Cool Million*—a shadow of what is to come in his last work—he captures the restless frustration, hostility, and indiscriminate capacity for violence of the crowd:

> Before Mr. Whipple had quite finished his little talk, the crowd ran off in all directions, shouting "Lynch him! Lynch him!" although a good three-quarters of its members did not know whom it was they were supposed to lynch. This fact did not bother them, however. They considered their lack of knowledge an advantage rather than a hindrance, for it gave them a great deal of leeway in their choice of a victim.
>
> Those of the mob who were better informed made for the opera house. . . . Feeling that they ought to hang somebody, the crowd put a rope around Jake Raven's neck because of his dark complexion. They then fired the building.
>
> . . . . .
>
> Other, more practical-minded citizens proceeded to rob the bank and loot the principal stores. . . .

> As time went on, the riot grew more general. . . . The heads of negroes were paraded on poles. A Jewish drummer was nailed to the door of his hotel room. The housekeeper of the local Catholic priest was raped. (pp. 245-46)

In West's last three novels, the main characters act out their roles against an ominous mass of shadowy, broken, violent people. This crowd, which in *The Day of the Locust* occasionally steps from behind a darkened curtain into West's grotesque spotlight, never does so in *A Cool Million*. One never feels its presence as intensely as one does in his last work. Nevertheless, West has continued his vague analysis of the American anonymous crowd begun in *Miss Lonelyhearts*.

At the heart of West's analysis is the belief that illusions, if not more terrible than lack of illusions, are certainly more dangerous when unchecked by introspection. Trapped by a set of beliefs which have little relation to reality, the masses are seething with frustration, the cause of which they do not understand. Lacking insight into the origin of their malaise, and hence unable to combat it, they are prone to violent aggression when a scapegoat appears on the scene. West's analysis of the mentality of such crowds is sketchy in *A Cool Million*. But while valid only for unintrospective societies—and so somewhat less valid for "sophisticated" post–World War II America than for pre–World War II America—his interpretation is still extremely suggestive.

West implies that depression America, like depression Europe, was schizoid. Two divergent forces were at work: idealism and resentment. The inevitable conflict between these antagonistic tendencies is aggravated by the crowd's inability and lack of desire to fathom the forces at work upon it. The result is a savage sense of betrayal that must erupt in violence. All that is needed to unleash it is an object—a scapegoat—or an excuse. The schizoid nature of the crowd, however, makes it essential that the aggression meet with its conscious—idealistic—self-approval. This is the paradox: the violence, just as in Nazi Germany, must be committed in the name of idealism. Thus, almost all of Whipple's appeals are idealistic ones: "freedom," "jobs," "the general good of the country."

It is difficult to understand why West might have abandoned the tone of *Miss Lonelyhearts* in order to return to the tone of

Balso Snell. Perhaps it was personal involvement, or perhaps an intuitive sense that he was striking too close to a "mass neurosis." Whatever the cause, West not only has prevented his audience from becoming indignant at the accuracy of the analysis, he has prevented them from taking it seriously enough to examine its accuracy. Much of the reader's failure to be engaged is due to the extremism of West's portrait; such extremism is useful only if it helps to make a point. It is quite another matter when the reflection is so extreme that it prevents one from seeing the original object. And this West has done. One is so amused by America as West presents it that one is neither frightened nor angered by it. In essence, one chuckles at the carnival mirror—a hearty chuckle, with a guffaw here and there—but the reflection is of no importance. For after all, who takes carnival mirrors seriously? No one. And that is the point. On first and casual reading—the most one can and should ask of the reader of *A Cool Million*—no one can take it seriously enough. As a result, the novel fails. If it fails as a "novel of ideas," it fails entirely; for it is not a "novel of character" and was never meant to be.

Though a failure, the novel is an interesting one. In it, the steady enlargement of West's focus continues. Where *Balso Snell* is extremely personal, and *Miss Lonelyhearts* only slightly less so, with *A Cool Million* West begins his detached dissection of society, a dissection which culminates in *The Day of the Locust.* In a sense, *A Cool Million* is an unintentional but perhaps necessary exercise for that last novel; for, in the process of debunking the American myth, West learned to examine the victims of that myth. In his last novel, the usual transposition from comic to serious again occurs: no longer comic, in *The Day of the Locust* the victims are sinister. Yet, in a very real sense, in *A Cool Million,* West's interest in the victims has not yet been aroused; he is concerned with the victimizers, and concerned with them in a narrow political and economic way. The shift to the "lower depths" and the enlargement of his analysis to include social and psychological factors indicate a deepening in West's pessism. Though West has not yet reached the pessimism of his last novel, he has already begun to take on the prophet's robe: the period of warning has begun. At first West is conjectural; later he is emphatic. Thus, *A Cool Million* is a warning of what might be; *The Day of the Locust*, a vision of what is. The warning in this novel to beware before it is too late becomes, five depression years later, a warning that it already may be too late.

Interesting as *A Cool Million* may be in helping to chart West's development as thinker and artist, it is hardly one of the "most undeservedly neglected"[4] books of the past twenty-five years. On the contrary, with Balso one is tempted to say: "Interesting psychologically, but is it art?"

The novel is at times genuinely funny, but all that is unique and fine in West is lacking: the tension between the intellect and the emotions, the smouldering intensity. These, always dependent on West's peculiar image of man, on his style, and on his own ambiguous attitude toward "Westian man," are missing; and by detaching himself from his usual concern with all three, he has emasculated his writing. West must have sensed something of this, for in *The Day of the Locust* he returns with a vengeance to his early concerns and earlier figurative and symbolical manner.

VII. *The Day of the Locust*

The Day of the Locust is unlike any other novel West wrote: something not altogether unexpected, for all of West's novels are highly original. Thus, *Balso Snell* is a picaresque farce in a surrealist manner; *Miss Lonelyhearts,* a moving, comic satire bordering on Sophoclean tragedy; *A Cool Million,* a rollicking picaresque satire after the fashion of Horatio Alger. But how does one describe *The Day of the Locust*? Stylistically it resembles *Miss Lonelyhearts,* but structurally it bears little resemblance to West's other novels. Moreover, it differs from the other novels by failing to focus indignation upon any single aspect of existence. *Balso Snell* is, among other things, "a protest against writing books"; *Miss Lonelyhearts,* a protest against man's inadequacy to solve, and pretense at having solved, the metaphysical "facts of life"; and *A Cool Million,* an attack against the dangers of Americanism. After completing each of these novels, the reader comes away with a fairly precise impression of the author's intended statement: art is false and dangerous; man is helpless to understand or change the "laws of life," and any attempt to delude himself to the contrary leads to destruction; uncritical Americanism is one step away from fascism. For present purposes, it is not important that one agree with the author's central statement; what is important is that one is able to formulate it. In *The Day of the Locust,* one finds it difficult to crystallize in one's mind the central point of the novel. In many respects, the reader's inability to do so comprises the major failing of the novel.

Much has been made of the apparent "coolness" of *The Day of the Locust;* while many factors, such as West's detachment,[1] might explain this lack of life and warmth, it seems to originate as much in reader misunderstanding as in anything West may or may not have done. There are, of course, aspects of the novel which might make it seem to lack warmth when compared to *Miss Lonelyhearts.*

In *Miss Lonelyhearts,* the horror in the novel is dramatized by means of Miss Lonelyhearts' problem. The intense sense of identification West felt with his persona charges the novel with an electric atmosphere that is only periodically present in *The Day of the Locust.* Here it is only occasionally present because the horror is not restricted to Tod, the "Westian man"; because the persona is less a participant in the action than a spectator of it; because his problem is not *the* central drama of the novel; because the pervasiveness of the horror tends to diminish its impact; and, finally, because West's coolness and lifeless detachment is always greatest when he creates non-Westian grotesques. Sometimes the source of West's inspiration is chilling observation rather than introspection, and, unfortunately, much of *The Day of the Locust* has this chill. There is, however, a real sense in which *The Day of the Locust* is a misread novel. A remark by Hyman, ordinarily a most perceptive critic, is typical of the kind of critical reservation given the novel:

> Despite this [the riot scene] and other very powerful scenes, I think that *The Day of the Locust* ultimately fails as a novel. Shifting from Tod to Homer and back to Tod, it has no dramatic unity, and in comparison with *Miss Lonelyhearts,* it has no moral core. Where Miss Lonelyhearts' inability to stay in Betty's Eden is heartbreaking, Tod's disillusion with Faye is only sobering, and where the end of the former is tragic, the end of this, Tod in the police car screaming along with the siren, is merely hysteric.[2]

Hyman's remark suggests that, measured by conventional novelistic standards, it is a failure; and, indeed, when so measured it is a failure. But it is precisely by such standards that one must not judge the novel. Like *Miss Lonelyhearts, The Day of the Locust* is a symbolical novel; but unlike the earlier novel, *The Day of the Locust* is a dramatized world view, not a dramatized problem. It is a generalized vision of a world running down. Instead of focusing attention upon a single individual or upon a single motif, each episode in the novel is intent on revealing the spiritual malaise of contemporary society. *The Day of the Locust* is, and should be read as, a prose *Waste Land.* This is not to suggest that the novel is a translation into prose of that poem; however, it attempts to accomplish what the poem accomplished, and to accomplish it *in much the same way.* Nothing could render the novel greater injustice than a traditional, literal, narrative reading. The reader's concern should be with the feeling evoked by the symbolic detail, by the objective correlatives; for the brilliance of the novel lies in such symbolic impressions. In the face of such imagination and complexity, the failure of the novel to achieve the stature of *Miss Lonelyhearts* is not easy to explain; facile or superficial explanations are inadequate.

West's attempt to abstract and objectify the twentieth-century malaise instead of merely finding a symbol for it, as he does in *Miss Lonelyhearts,* is not in itself a normative matter. It does not determine the merit of the novel per se—that is essentially a matter of artistry. But West seems to have been at his best when most intimate, when working in miniature. Any enlargement of the canvas coarsened his fine finish and magnified his weaknesses. While the scope of his portrait placed obstacles in his path, West incorporated almost everything he had learned in his previous novels to surmount them.

Though *The Day of the Locust* is almost one-third again as long as *A Cool Million* and over twice as long as *Miss Lonelyhearts,* it is still a short novel, totaling little more than 160 pages in any of the various published editions. Even with an extremely spare style which permitted him to omit inessentials, West would have found it difficult to suggest all that he has about the wasteland and the malaise and still write a unified novel. Had West been content merely to write a novel about Hollywood, he might have succeeded in writing a work with the artistic unity of *Miss Lonelyhearts*—but he was attempting much more; he makes it clear that Hollywood is but a dramatic sore in a bleeding society:

> He [Tod] only wondered if he weren't exaggerating the importance of the people who come to California to die. Maybe they weren't really desperate enough to set a single city on fire, let alone the whole country. Maybe they were only the pick of America's madmen and not at all typical of the rest of the land. . . .
>
> Nevertheless, he refused to give up the role of Jeremiah. He changed "pick of America's madmen" to "cream" and felt almost

> certain that the milk from which it had been skimmed was just as rich in violence. . . . (*The Day of the Locust*, p. 78)

In an attempt to suggest something of this larger cancer, West employs a structure which, while not picaresque, superficially has more in common with *A Cool Million* than with *Miss Lonelyhearts*; in all other matters—tonal, stylistic—*The Day of the Locust* resembles the latter. The reason for such structure is not strange. Though there are a half-dozen central characters in *Miss Lonelyhearts,* from the moment Miss Lonelyhearts is introduced in the first sentence of the novel until the final line, he is in the foreground. In the way that Hamlet is the play, Miss Lonelyhearts is the novel. This is not true of *A Cool Million,* for the novel, despite its subtitle, is not really concerned with the narrow career of Lemuel Pitkin but with something larger: American society and Whipple as a reflection of that society. The dismantlement of Lemuel unifies the novel, but now and then Lem falls away from the foreground while West concerns himself with other matters.

This pattern understandably is even more evident in *The Day of the Locust.* Tod Hackett is the protagonist, but again there is a larger concern—those who had "come to California to die." While Tod is the central figure in the novel, he—like Lem—suggests less about the society than do Harry, Homer, and Faye. For this reason, the novel often concerns itself with explaining Homer and Harry and, to a lesser extent, Faye. Sometimes West merely shifts the center of focus of the novel from Tod to Homer, as he does in Chapters Eight through Twelve. More often than not, however, West chooses to filter the reader's knowledge of the others through Tod. Such a method serves to characterize Tod; but as a structural or even psychological matter, it is of incidental concern. What is important to West is that there is an intelligence commenting upon the events and the characters.

West must have realized the difficulty of dramatizing the disorder of an entire civilization, as well as the importance of brevity to his method. His only possible solution, then, was to create a commentator, and he brilliantly succeeded in doing so. Tod not only is a commentator, he is fundamentally involved in the action of the novel. So well does West handle this problem that at first glance one may neglect to notice that Tod's comments pervade the novel.[3] Part of our failure to become preoccupied with Tod as spectator is due to the construction of the novel and to the nature of the comments themselves.

The novel is conceived in such a fashion that it can be quite easily viewed as a revelation of Tod's character; such is the prevalent and, it seems likely, erroneous way of viewing it. From this perspective, Tod's comments are not only natural but necessary if one is to have more than a passing appreciation of his character. Such "deception" takes artistry, but it is deception, for the novel is not meant to be primarily a revelation of Tod's character —it is meant to be precisely the opposite. In addition to this deception, however, West forms Tod's commentary with a penetration and precision that removes it from sociology and raises it to poetry.

Thus, after describing the "plaster, lath and paper" houses of the Hollywood hills, "the Mexican ranch houses, Samoan huts, Mediterranean villas, Egyptian and Japanese temples, Swiss chalets, Tudor cottages . . ." and particularly, "a Rhine Castle" and "a little highly colored shack with domes and minarets out of the *Arabian Nights*," he has Tod make a transition from response to commentary:

> He was charitable. Both houses were comic, but he didn't laugh. Their desire to startle was so eager and guileless.
>
> It is hard to laugh at the need for beauty and romance, no matter how tasteless, even horrible, the results of that need are. But it is easy to sigh. Few things are sadder than the truly monstrous. (p. 4)

This transition helps to disguise the commentary, and West uses the device repeatedly. In another example, Tod is reflecting upon "a gigantic pile of sets, flats and props":

> This was the final dumping ground. . . . Many boats sink and never reach the Sargasso, but no dream ever entirely disappears. Somewhere it troubles some unfortunate person and some day, when that person has been sufficiently troubled, it will be reproduced on the lot. (p. 97)

This passage is sufficiently close to direct commentary to merit almost the name; but passages of completely direct commentary occur frequently enough to warrant separate attention. Such commentary is not usual in West—it occurs in this fashion in no other novel—but the frequency with which it does occur makes one question the accuracy of Richard B. Gehman's remark that "When *The Day of the Locust* finally came out, it was apparent that West had learned to let his characters and scenes make their own points without his intrusion";[4] or Alan Ross' that "*The Day of the Locust* is his [West's] most mature [work] because in it his criticism of life is not intruding between the characters";[5] for this is exactly what does seem to happen. Thus, his description of Homer Simpson contains such passages as the following:

> Between the sun, the lizard and the house, he was fairly well occupied. But whether he was happy or not it is hard to say. Probably he was neither . . . (p. 41)
>
> . . . . .
>
> There are men who can lust with parts of themselves. Only their brain or their hearts burn and then not completely. There are others, still more fortunate, who are like filaments of an incandescent lamp. They burn fiercely, yet nothing is destroyed. But in Homer's case it would be like dropping a spark into a barn full of hay. (pp. 56-57)

Such comments—unfairly emphasized by being isolated from the text—might be disturbing (and the first one is) if they were not so brief and suggestive. They do indicate clearly that there is no significant normative difference between the way West makes his points or presents his criticism of life in *Miss Lonelyhearts* and in *The Day of the Locust.* If anything, he intrudes less in *Miss Lonelyhearts*; in that novel he does not have to intrude. The essential difference between the two novels is that whereas the created characters of Shrike and Miss Lonelyhearts (but, significantly, not Betty) are such that their respective roles organically develop all of the novel's major themes, the themes of *The Day of the Locust* develop not nearly so organically. The intention of the novel requires a different developmental technique. A vision of the aimless disorder of modern existence is only possible when viewed whole, as, for example, by a Tiresias—"a mere spectator."

Despite the fact that Tiresias is "not indeed a 'character'" in *The Waste Land,* Eliot still calls him "the most important personage in the poem, uniting all the rest."[6] Tod, though no Tiresias, is the seer of *The Day of the Locust,* and he must be seen in this role of spectator and unifier if one is to read the novel rightly. West is not reticent in pointing out to the reader that Tod is the observer and interpreter of the action.

About halfway through the novel, Tod identifies himself with the prophet Jeremiah. This identification merely lends an added historical and archetypal dimension to Tod's role, which has been given to the reader in the beginning of the novel:

> From the moment he had seen them [the people who had come to California to die], he had known that, despite his race, training and heritage, neither Winslow Homer nor Thomas Ryder could be his masters and he turned to Goya and Daumier. (p. 3)

In naming his new masters, Tod indicates that he has forsaken decorative art for social criticism. Periodically, West reminds the reader of Tod's concern. During his visit to the studio, where "Waterloo" is being filmed, he begins to reflect:

> He had lately begun to think not only of Goya and Daumier but also of certain Italian artists of the seventeenth and eighteenth centuries, of Salvator Rosa, Francesco Guardi and Monsu Desiderio, the painters of Decay and Mystery. (p. 96)

His painting, "The Burning of Los Angeles," is a surrealist fusion of the prophet and the artist. Moreover, his description of how he will paint the crowd offers a clue to the style of *The Day of the Locust* itself:

> As he watched these people writhe on the hard seats of their churches, he thought of how well Alessandro Magnasco would dramatize the contrast between their drained-out, feeble bodies and their wild, disordered minds. He would not satirize them as Hogarth or Daumier might, nor would he pity them. He would paint their fury with respect. . . . (p. 109)

If what Tod sees is not exactly "the substance"[7] of the novel, it is the largest part of it. West's conception of the novel demanded that he filter his insights through the mind of a seer, for in only such a way could he sharpen the symbolic detail of the novel. Moreover, if in *Miss Lonelyhearts* West merely used his protagonist to suggest the "decline of the West," in *The Day of the Locust* he is concerned with a more comprehensive analysis of that decline. West attempted to convey so much in his last novel that it was impossible for him to allow his characters to speak for themselves and to characterize themselves completely through action and dialogue.

In reading the novel, however, one hardly notices this shorthand method of characterizing, perhaps because of the swiftness of the portrait itself. The events of the novel—the reader's impressions of the characters themselves—follow upon each other too rapidly for him to analyze the fashion in which an effect is created. West had used the same method, with the same result, in *Miss Lonelyhearts*. But the manner in which he accelerates the movement of the novel and still suggests character and relationships is even finer here.

With the exception of passages such as those above and the sketchiest of descriptive passages, West reveals character through interrelationships. The method can be illustrated better by focusing attention on the swiftness with which West captures the essence of Tod's relationship with Faye Greener. These are the first comments made about Faye:

> He paused for a moment on the landing of the second [floor]. It was on that floor that Faye Greener lived, in 208. When someone laughed in one of the apartments he started guiltily and continued upstairs. (p. 4)
>
> . . . . .
>
> He began to think of "honest Abe Kusich" in order not to think of Faye Greener. He felt comfortable and wanted to remain that way. (p. 5)
>
> . . . . .
>
> Tod allowed himself to be bullied and went with the dwarf to Pinyon Canyon. The rooms in the San Berdoo were small and not very clean. He rented one without hesitation, however, when he saw Faye Greener in the hall. (p. 11)

Only after these comments—and they are but part of a chapter on Tod's relationship with the dwarf—is an entire chapter devoted to developing Tod's relationship with Faye Greener.[8] These passages not only are suspense-provoking "plants," they already suggest, with tremendous economy, a complex attitude. West's choice of words and his juxtaposition of images create this effect.

Guilt, inner conflict, discomfort, and abject servitude are all suggested, and by the end of the chapter, the reader, too, is preoccupied with Faye Greener. It is only after subtle but careful preparation of this sort has been made that West presents him with a detailed account of Faye and Tod's relationship. Even as early as Chapter Three, West charges casual events with a significance that leads appropriately into his main discussion:

> He took a bath and shaved, then dressed in front of the bureau mirror. He tried to watch his fingers as he fixed his collar and tie, but his eyes kept straying to the photograph that was pushed into the upper corner of the frame.
>
> It was a picture of Faye Greener, a still from a two reel farce in which she had worked as an extra.
>
> . . . . .
>
> She was supposed to look drunk and she did, but not with alcohol. She lay stretched out on the divan with her arms and legs spread, as though welcoming a lover, and her lips were parted in a heavy, sullen smile. She was supposed to look inviting, but the invitation wasn't to pleasure.
>
> Tod lit a cigarette and inhaled with a nervous gasp. He started to fool with his tie again, but had to go back to the photograph.
>
> Her invitation wasn't to pleasure, but to struggle, hard and sharp, closer to murder than to love. If you threw yourself on her, it would be like throwing yourself from the parapet of a skyscraper. You would do it with a scream. You couldn't expect to rise again. Your teeth would be driven into your skull like nails into a pine board and your back would be broken. You wouldn't even have time to sweat or close your eyes.
>
> He managed to laugh at his language, but it wasn't a real laugh and nothing was destroyed by it. (pp. 11-12)

In this passage, one finds the same high finish that stamped *Miss Lonelyhearts:* the ear for the suggestive phrase, the eye for detail, the brilliant images, the ability to create intensity and layers of meaning through trivial events like tying a tie or lighting a cigarette, and, finally, the self-conscious, barking laugh that is the mark of Westian man. It is a passage typical of the prose in *The Day of the Locust,* prose that is every bit as fine as that in *Miss Lonelyhearts.* The dialogue, always good in West, is even better than the dialogue in *Miss Lonelyhearts* because more central, varied, and vital. Nor can one take exception to the figurative language in *The Day of the Locust,* for it is every bit as rich and profuse as it is in *Miss Lonelyhearts:*

> She was leaning toward him, drooping slightly, but not from fatigue.[9] He had seen young birches droop like that at midday when they are over-heavy with sun. (*Ibid.*, p. 89)
>
> . . . . .
>
> He had the same countersunk eyes, like the heads of burnished spikes, that a monk by Magnasco might have. (*Ibid.*, p. 110)
>
> . . . . .
>
> He cried without covering his face or bending his head. The sound was like an ax chopping pine, a heavy, hollow chunking noise. It was repeated rhythmically but without accent. There was no progress in it. Each chunk was exactly like the one that preceded. It would never reach climax. (*Ibid.*, p. 143)

Yet, despite the power of West's description in *The Day of the Locust,* his ability to retell a story, and his variety, in the end one still feels the novel to be inferior to *Miss Lonelyhearts.* Light has attributed this inferiority to the "greater ambitiousness" of the novel, with its resultant "rambling" loss of direction, and to a defect in "West's choice of viewpoint." To these reasons Light also attributes the "difference in warmth of the novels [*Miss Lonelyhearts* and *The Day of the Locust*]." He ends his analysis of the matter with the following remark:

> . . . at times in *The Day* there is the feeling that the sigh with which West views "the truly monstrous" (p. 4) is just a trifle cold, as if the fear engendered by the starers were slowly turning the pity of the author into hysteria, disgust, and even hatred. This may have been the effect that West intended, but more likely he wished to gain an effect similar to that of *Miss Lonelyhearts.*[10]

More than likely, West was not trying to achieve an effect similar to *Miss Lonelyhearts*—at least no more so than Eliot in *The Waste Land* was trying to achieve an effect similar to "The Love Song of J. Alfred Prufrock." Prophetic visions are not famed for compassion. West, like Tod, refused to satirize or pity the people in *The Day of the Locust,* whereas the very excellence of *Miss Lonelyhearts* exists precisely in an almost perfect tonal fusion of the two.

Though correct in suggesting that *The Day of the Locust* "is not as perfect a book as *Miss Lonelyhearts*," and largely correct in his attempted explanation, Light errs in ascribing the novel's relative inferiority to "a weakness in his [West's] art"; it is not lack of art that weakens the novel but faulty judgment. West failed to realize that those intangible qualities—apart from style and character—which made him such a fine writer were tension and intensity. These he sacrificed by writing a novel which lacks focus, brevity, and unity.

When West is basically serious—as he is in *Miss Lonelyhearts* and *The Day of the Locust,* and as he is not in *Balso Snell* and *A Cool Million*—his novels are rooted in tension and charged with intensity. From the beginning the reader is treading on high-voltage wire. The result is an impression of power; he is brought almost immediately to a state of great emotional agitation. West forces this heightened state on the reader by seizing upon a neurotic response which reveals the feverish intensity of his grotesques. Often this intensity is revealed merely by pointing out a disparity between stimulus and response: Miss Lonelyhearts staring furiously at a cigarette that refuses to draw; the crowd's eyes filling with hatred when their stare is returned. Such initial intensity, increased by the force of West's personality and style, is an asset; but it presents him with problems. Even if he can sustain, or worse, increase such great emotional excitement—and it is doubtful that he can in a novel of any great length—can the reader support it? It is unlikely. The result is an occasional letdown which the reader may magnify. Without quite understanding what has happened, the reader is liable to feel that the novel is spotty or uneven.

The problem of intensity can largely be circumvented and the power left undiminished if certain conditions are met: (1) If the novel is short enough: *Miss Lonelyhearts* is seventy-five pages long in *The Complete Works*—an hour's reading; *The Day of the Locust*—West's longest novel—is over twice that length—not short enough. (2) If the novel preserves a single center of focus: *Miss Lonelyhearts* does; *The Day of the Locust* does not. (3) If the conflict remains simple and basic, as in *Miss Lonelyhearts*; and if it does not shift from internal to external conflict as well as from central—Tod and Faye—to peripheral conflicts—Tod and Earle, Faye and Harry, Homer and Faye—as it does in *The Day of the Locust.* (4) If the novel preserves its unity: *Miss Lonelyhearts* has the concentration of a Sophoclean tragedy; *The Day of the Locust,* little, if any.

It is strange that West, who once remarked, "Lyric novels can be written according to Poe's definition of a lyric poem,"[11] should have forgotten this one of Poe's major esthetic principles. There are possibilities available to *The Waste Land,* which is scarcely more than four hundred lines, that are not available to a novel the length of West's, which is simply too long to create a single overpowering effect. Instead, it leaves one moved and impressed by a series of vivid but somehow disjointed scenes; one is unable to perceive their over-all coherence. A feeling of diffuseness and lack of compression results, and the novel fails to impress one with the power of an executioner's axe; instead, it leaves a series of vivid hatchet marks, each one clean and incisive. But the one blow in *Miss Lonelyhearts* finishes the reader; all those in *The Day of the Locust* (with the possible exception of the last) do not. The power of West's novels is not increased by an *accumulation* of various scenes of power but by scenes of power that are *incremental,* increasing the *single* powerful movement of the novel until it crashes to its inevitable close. The riot scene at the end of *The Day of the Locust* is so effective because it alone has incremental force; it alone is the inevitable violent end of all that has gone before.

Perhaps West intuitively realized the virtue of incremental as opposed to accumulated power, for in matters of fundamental concern, such as the crowd, he is faithful to this incremental pattern. Unfortunately, because the crowd is only a part of this generalized vision of horror, it is often allowed to fade into the background. These "hollow men" are never allowed to disappear, however; for only against a backdrop of maimed, wasted shadows do the apparently random actions of the main actors take on their full significance as correlatives of a massive modern disintegration. If the reader fails to understand this fact, fails to perceive the symbolic nature of the action, and fails to see that West has made a concerted effort to show the interrelatedness of the central characters and the crowd, he has failed to understand either the structure or the meaning of the novel. Such, however, is an understandable failure, for *The Day of the Locust* is West's most complex novel, and the one which contains all of the diverse elements of his world view. Thus, the themes of his first three novels —illusions *vs.* reality, dreams, acting and identity, honesty, self-consciousness, sex, and the crowd, among others—all find expression in his last novel.

Just as in *Balso Snell*, West in *The Day of the Locust* is concerned with how illusions and acting corrupt genuine feeling. As in all his previous novels, he is dealing with the disparity between illusions and reality, but with one significant difference: he fails to develop this theme or any other through irony. Moreover, with the exception of a few ironic remarks, the novel is almost devoid of irony. Even apparent ironies, such as the actor becoming the part played, are scarcely ironic. It is difficult to understand the reason for West's abandonment of the ironic mode. Perhaps he felt that the subject matter demanded "respect." Whatever the reason for this tonal departure, it results in a loss of wry warmth, and in a chilling directness unusual in West.

The humor of the novel helps to moderate these effects a bit, for it is frequent and varied. Some of it arises out of Hollywood's gaudy incongruities: drugstore "Indians" with Yiddish accents (p. 150); or out of West's ability to inform Faye's card file of dreams, Tod's dream rape of Faye, and "Le Prédicament de Marie" with an amusing clichéd reality. Most of it, however, arises out of West's ear for dialogue, as when he captures the truculent vulgarity of Abe Kusich's speech: "'Some gal!' [said Tod.] 'You bet,' said the dwarf. 'A lollapalooza—all slut and a yard wide. . . . No quiff can give Abe Kusich the fingeroo and get away with it'" (p. 7); the prurient caterwauling of Mrs. Schwartzen: "'Are you talking smut? . . . I adore smut. . . . Go ahead, do say something obscene'" (pp. 14-15); the wooden conversation of "criminally handsome" Earle and his cowboy friends which consists essentially of "Lo thar"; or the involved, comic rhetoric of Claude Estee:

> "Love is like a vending machine, eh? Not bad. You insert a coin and press home the lever. There's some mechanical activity inside the bowels of the device. You receive a small sweet, frown at yourself in the dirty mirror, adjust your hat, take a firm grip on your umbrella and walk away, trying to look as though nothing happened. It's good, but it's not for pictures." (pp. 17-18)

All of this helps dissipate some of the chill surrounding the novel; but, for the most part, the humor lacks the robust vigor of Shrike's rhetoric. It is too transparently sad. There is too much defeat bordering on despair in Claude's voice, too much pathos in Abe Kusich. Moreover, nothing could withstand the terrible shadow of the crowd that blankets the book from beginning to end.

The Day of the Locust opens, like *Miss Lonelyhearts,* with a brilliant chapter containing most of the novel's motifs. Many of them are uniquely West's, but many suggest the influence of Eliot. It is unlikely that West used Eliot's poem as a source book; however, the similarity of the two works becomes clear when one perceives how remarkably appropriate this description of *The Waste Land* is to *The Day of the Locust:*

> Eliot sees the contemporary world as deaf and blind to the realities behind the old symbols and myths of its literary tradition and therefore stunted and parched in its whole emotional living. The central symbol of the fragmentariness, the moral ugliness, and the boredom of the contemporary scene is the modern City. It represents the lack of fertility and communion between man and God, between man and man, between man and woman, and between man and his traditional cultural heritage.[12]

As he had in *Miss Lonelyhearts,* West introduces his protagonist immediately; but unlike Miss Lonelyhearts, Tod, almost from the first sentence, is portrayed as a spectator. Tod hurries to the window of his office: "An army of cavalry and foot was passing. It moved like a mob; its line broken, as though fleeing from some terrible defeat" (p. 1). Actually, it is fleeing from the little fat man. With this grotesque opening incongruity, the note of falseness that runs throughout the novel is established, as well as the ugly reality underlying appearances.

A little later, Tod examines the evening Hollywood crowd. Almost like a set piece before the dramatic action begins, the first chapter presents the two Hollywoods, the "dream dump" and the land of dead dreams. In his image of the people who stare, and in his description of the "masquerades" and of the houses "that lined the slopes of the canyon," West swiftly and garishly captures the modern city with its boredom, riotous ugliness, and lack of individual or cultural identity.

Apathy's counterpart, lechery, is introduced in the second chapter. Abe Kusich has just been thrown out of a "slut's" apartment. He is appalled by her lack of gratitude: " 'Who gave her forty bucks for an abortion?' " (p. 10)

The entire novel dramatically and symbolically reworks the themes of these two chapters. Originally entitled *The Cheated* (Claude, significantly, was the commentator),[13] the novel explores the futility and anarchy of modern life, the modern spiritual malaise wherein, contrary to the opinion of most social critics, there are no cheaters—only cheated—and Hollywood is their home. West's selection of Hollywood is a happy choice, for from the first, Hollywood is presented as the "Unreal City."[14] West's description of the city and the crowd has all of the appearances of being straight out of Baudelaire: "Swarming city, city full of dreams,/ Where the specter in broad daylight accosts the passer-by."[15]

Time and again West universalizes the city; he also emphasizes its unreality. It is impossible to avoid believing that West had Eliot in mind when he created the atmosphere of the opening chapter, for his description of Hollywood echoes Eliot's description and catalog of unreal cities in *The Waste Land,* even to the "violet light" that bathes the city:[16]

> The edges of the trees burned with a pale violet light and their centers gradually turned from deep purple to black. The same violet piping, like a Neon tube, outlined the tops of the ugly, hump-backed hills. . . . (p. 3)

Tod's comments further universalize the city. Musing upon the significance of the crowd, he begins to generalize. He toys with, but rejects, the notion that his specters were "only the pick of America's madmen"; he feels "almost certain that . . . the Angelenos would be first, but their comrades all over the country would follow" (p. 78). Viewing the "awful, anarchic power" of his torchbearers, he is "aware that they had it in them to destroy civilization" (p. 100).

The novel abounds in artistic, historical, and biblical allusions. As Tod watches "people writhe on the hard seats of their churches," he speculates on "how well Alessandro Magnasco would dramatize the contrast between their drained-out, feeble bodies and their wild, disordered minds" (p. 109). In the "Tabernacle of the Third Coming," a man stands up to speak:

> He was very angry. The message he had brought to the city was one that an illiterate anchorite might have given decadent Rome. . . . He claimed to have seen the Tiger of Wrath stalking the walls of the citadel and the Jackal of Lust skulking in the shrubbery. . . . (p. 110)

Passing through a studio lot, Tod reflects on the meaning of Hollywood:

> He thought of Janvier's "Sargasso Sea." Just as that imaginary body of water was a history of civilization in the form of a marine junkyard, the studio lot was one in the form of a dream dump. A sargasso of the imagination! (p. 97)

Hollywood is merely a dramatic symbol of a generalized attempt to disguise the barrenness of modern life. It is an unsuccessful attempt; hence the feeling of having been cheated. Nevertheless, so pervasive is the city's corrupting influence that —with the perennial exceptions of Earle, and Miguel the human cock—all of the characters have been forced to assume various poses.

In this characteristic, as in their desire to escape, the characters are all of a piece. West obviously desired such an effect, for throughout the novel he takes pains to relate the action going on in the foreground to the action in the background—to dramatize the essential unity of the characters and the crowd. The unity is developed by indirect commentary and by the use of leitmotifs—apathy, lechery, frustration, violence, flight—the most pervasively developed one being the flight motif.

In many ways, Tod's enslavement to Faye is one form of escape, just as the crowd's vicarious existence, Faye's dreams, Harry's acting, and Homer's sleep are others, but with one difference: Tod is aware of his dynamics, the others are not.

> He began to wonder if he himself didn't suffer from the ingrained, morbid apathy he liked to draw in others. Maybe he could only be galvanized into sensibility and that was why he was chasing Faye. (p. 109)

To this explanation, West adds another which forces one to

perceive the fundamental unity of all the characters in *The Day of the Locust,* with the exception of Earle and Mig, who are merely part of the garish Hollywood landscape:

> He was interested in Harry and enjoyed visiting him. The old man was a clown and Tod had all the painter's usual love of clowns. But what was more important, he felt that his clownship was a clue to the people who stared (a painter's clue, that is—a clue in the form of a symbol), just as Faye's dreams were another. (pp. 23-24)

The clue, of course, is that Harry's clownship is "his sole method of defense," just as Faye's dreams, Claude's jokes, Homer's chastity, and Tod's enslavement are theirs. The defense is against reality—the great cheat.

West's characters play out their defenses and escapes with a hysterical desperation. Even Faye, who is only seventeen, is aware of the dead dreams around her. Though she is seemingly lost in a world of dreams, her remark about her "method" suggests that she is not unaware of the nature of the reality she is fleeing:

> She would get some music on the radio, then lie down on her bed and shut her eyes. She had a large assortment of stories to choose from. After getting herself in the right mood, she would go over them in her mind, as though they were a pack of cards. . . .
>
> While she admitted that her method was too mechanical for the best results and that it was better to slip into a dream naturally, she said that any dream was better than no dream and beggers couldn't be choosers. (p. 60)

But the meaning of her flight is lost to her: "Her critical powers ended there. She only smiled at the mechanics" (p. 60).

If Faye represents the born dreamer in society, Homer represents the sleeper. In being psychosexual, his apathy is like that of the crowd; and like the crowd's, it too culminates in violence. Fearing that even this correspondence would be inadequate, West, already having suggested the other characters' link to the crowd, is explicit in establishing Homer's shortly afterward. It is accomplished as soon as he is introduced:

> Tod examined him [Homer] eagerly. He didn't mean to be rude but at first glance this man seemed an exact model for the

kind of person who comes to California to die, perfect in every detail down to fever eyes and unruly hands.

. . . . .

Tod saw that he was mistaken. Homer Simpson was only physically the type. The men he meant were not shy. (p. 27)

Tod is not entirely mistaken, however, as West makes clear on the very next page: "Tod was right about one thing at least. Like most of the people he was interested in, Homer was a Middle-Westerner." By the end of *The Day of the Locust,* more than this passing identification has been established. Homer becomes a symbolic abstraction of the crowd. Devoid of imagination, Homer of all the major characters is the only one who is unable to adopt poses—poses which are the others' major defense.

These poses are played out against a tableau of dead souls. They are the victims who populate the dead dream world of Hollywood. Surrounding these "poor bastards," but also surrounding everyone in the novel, is an unbearable physical and spiritual isolation. Always a central concern in West, the isolation that results from a failure to communicate is unbearably oppressive in *The Day of the Locust.* Heartbreaking in *Miss Lonelyhearts,* here it is horrifying. Communication is impossible, and alienation, common to all of West's protagonists with the exception of Lem Pitkin, is general. From top to bottom, the isolation of the characters has resulted in blunted sensibility. The result at the bottom is the "vicious, acrid boredom that trembled on the edge of violence" (p. 91), but the affective stupor is general.

If those who had "come to California to die" image the deadness at the bottom, Claude Estee dramatizes the polite apathy at the top. He pretends that he has the "Epicurean belly," the expansive laugh and good-natured wit that accompanies *joie de vivre;* but, in reality, he is "a dried up little man" whose laughter is forced and whose wit ends in a sigh of regret.

His parties reproduce in miniature the pretense and fraud of Hollywood. He does an impersonation of a Civil War colonel which is in keeping with the style of his home, an "exact reproduction of the Old Dupuy Mansion near Biloxi, Mississippi." In reply to a shout for drinks—" 'Here, you black rascal! A mint julep!' "—a "Chinese servant" brings "Scotch and soda" (p. 13). For fun Claude plants a rubber imitation dead horse in his swimming pool. The men talking shop have other ideas of fun: they speculate on the place of charity in Hollywood.

> "They [the movie moguls] ought to put some of the millions they make back into the business again. Like Rockefeller does with his Foundation. People used to hate the Rockefellers, but now instead of hollering about their ill-gotten oil dough, everybody praises them for what the Foundation does. It's a swell stunt and pictures could do the same thing. Have a Cinema Foundation and make contributions to Science and Art. You know, give the racket a front." (p. 17)

The top is a wasteland as terrible as the bottom. But twisting the triteness of this possible cliché, West shows that money allows these people to indulge their whims. They do not "watch the waves come in at Venice," they watch "Le Prédicament de Marie." Though cheated too, they do not "burn with resentment"; their indignation is tepid. A bland regret that never quite becomes despair is all they can manage.

Unlike those at the top, who are incapable of almost all feeling, Harry Greener, at the bottom, is incapable of almost all genuine feeling. The theatrical pose becomes congenital: a prolonged excursion into the realm of artifice has resulted in a loss of familiarity with the real. Harry has been dispossessed of his personality—of his identity—through disuse. Only Harry's congenital posture prevents him from disintegrating; but when he is "really sick," the iron mask that hides his emotional scars falls away. "The last block that held him poised over the runway of self-pity had been knocked away and he was sliding down the chute, gaining momentum all the time." But the habits of a lifetime are too strong—the person has become the pose:

> He jumped to his feet and began doing Harry Greener, poor Harry, honest Harry, well-meaning, humble, deserving, a good husband, a model father, a faithful Christian, a loyal friend.
>
> . . . . .
>
> At the end of his pantomine . . . he lay on the couch with his eyes closed and his chest heaving. He was even more surprised than Homer. (p. 43)

Harry's courageous pose is less disguise than self-deception and lack of recognition:

> "You okay now, Pop?"
>
> "Fine and dandy, baby, Right as rain, fit as a fiddle and lively as a flea, as the feller says."
>
> . . . . .
>
> Faye helped him over to the table. He tried to disguise how weak he was by doing an exaggerated Negro shuffle.
>
> Homer opened a can of sardines and sliced some bread. Harry smacked his lips over the food, but ate slowly and with an effort. (pp. 53-54)

Harry is an extreme example of the consequences of affectation on one's personality. He is the most dramatic example of those who must torture feeling from their corrupted bones at any expense. Like every other character in the novel, Harry must artificially stimulate feeling. To feel, he must act. This would be a grotesque ironic joke—the actor who acts so long that only the actor remains—if it were not for the darkness of the alternatives. As in all of West's novels, there is no escape. The "no exit" theme begun in the bowels of the Trojan horse and continued in Shrike's rhetoric and Miss Lonelyhearts' catatonic stupor is continued and generalized here. Acting corrupts feeling, as it does in Harry Greener, but reality deadens it—as it does in those who "had come to California to die."

If Harry has become incapable of genuine feeling because he has acted too long and too much, Faye has been incapacitated because of her dreams. Lost in her dreamy swamp, Faye seems to represent the cheating dream dump. Repeatedly she is described as the personification of deception:

> She repaid him for his compliment by smiling in a peculiar, secret way and running her tongue over her lips. It was one of her most characteristic gestures and very effective. It seemed to promise all sorts of undefined intimacies, yet it was really as simple and automatic as the word thanks. (p. 130)
>
> . . . . .
>
> This elaborate gesture, like all her others, was . . . completely meaningless, almost formal. . . . (p. 47)

In a final figure, her symbolic role is made clear:

> Faye's affectations, however, were so completely artificial that he found them charming.

> Being with her was like being backstage during an amateurish, ridiculous play. . . . (p. 59)

Tod is forgiving, and understandably so, for he realizes that Faye is victim as well as victimizer:

> She often recognized the falseness of an attitude, [but] she persisted in it because she didn't know how to be simpler or more honest. She was an actress who had learned from bad models in a bad school.
>
> . . . . .
>
> . . . [But] he had often seen her laugh at herself. What was more, he had even seen her laugh at her dreams. (pp. 59-60)

Faye's dreamy romanticism is a response to the emotional impoverishment of the contemporary wasteland. Her misfortune is to live in an age wherein men are either sensitive and impotent, or potent and insensitive. The Tarzan picture over her bed of "a beautiful young man with magnificent muscles" suggests her choice.

While Faye's dream-inducing method may be too "mechanical," West's control of symbolic overtones in the dream is not. The young girl in the dream is an obvious surrogate. More important, the dream has sexual overtones. The following passage is not only attitudinally revealing, it is clearly a projection of her fantasy wish:

> She becomes interested in a young sailor who is far below her in station, but very handsome. She flirts with him because she is bored. The sailor refuses to be toyed with . . . and tells her that he only takes orders from the captain. She gets sore as hell and threatens to have him fired, but he only laughs at her. . . . She falls in love with him, although maybe she doesn't realize it herself, because he is the first man who has ever said no to one of her whims. . . . (p. 62)

Faye's preoccupation with handsome men is understandable, if not excusable, in Hollywood; besides, intellectual depth is not one of Faye's strong characteristics. What is interesting about her dream is the contrast between the dominance of the dream male and the servility of the males surrounding her. (Significantly, only Mig and Earle sleep with her in the novel.) That much of her wish is sexual is suggested by the attack of the "big snake" on her surrogate while she is bathing naked. After her dream man "fights the snake for her and wins," he presumably takes the place of the snake.

Aside from a short working tour in Mrs. Jennings' discreet callhouse ("she would not let a girl of hers go to a man with whom she herself would not be willing to sleep" [p. 19]) in order to pay for her father's elaborate funeral, she sleeps with only two men.[17] It is of some symbolic interest that they are the keepers of the cocks.

The depth of West's pessimism and the immensity of his indictment are suggested by a realization that of all the characters in the novel, it is Faye whose sexual responses are, incredibly, the sanest and most wholesome. Sexual sanity is impossible in the "Unreal City," but compared to the other characters, she is neither apathetic nor lecherous; and in a world of half-men, promiscuity is paradoxically a pardonable quest. Moreover, though promiscuous, Faye is not indiscriminate. Tod may be uncertain of his motives for chasing Faye, but she is not at all uncertain why she will not sleep with him:

> He had nothing to offer her, neither money nor looks, and she could only love a handsome man and would only let a wealthy man love her. Tod was a "good-hearted man," and she liked "good-hearted men," but only as friends. She wasn't hard-boiled. It was just that she put love on a special plane, where a man without money or looks couldn't move. (p. 11)

What emerges clearly from this scene and throughout the novel is Faye's sexual vitality. Far from having a "wholesome" sexual attitude, Faye nevertheless possesses a responsiveness and a sense of the mystery of sex which differentiate her from the other characters in the novel. Faye, however, can hardly be called a sexual success; she is part of the pervasive sexual failure that is so depressing in the novel.

James T. Farrell has made a remark that superficially seems to be at odds with West's obsessive sexuality:

> He was fascinated by the grotesqueries of Hollywood. . . . Also, without being Puritan, there were things that he didn't like about the sexual behavior. . . . I recall him once remarking about some Hollywood people who would hire two prostitutes and take them into a hotel room at the same time.[18]

Robert Coates' remark, however, that "the garishness, etc., of Hollywood . . . satisfied his pessimistic outlook on life,"[19] explains West's fascination with those very aspects of existence which repelled him. For all West's sexuality, there is in him, as in Eliot, horror and disgust at the experience he depicts. If sexuality is pervasive in his works, it is because, like Eliot, West seizes upon sexual derangement as the most dramatic symptom of the failure of society to provide spiritual and emotional outlets. Hollywood was and is a place rich with examples. In this last novel, West finally finds the proper symbolical and sociological context in which to develop his obsession with sexuality. Every character in the novel is in one way or another sexually disordered. Always prone to sexual explanations of human behavior, West again seizes upon sexual disorder to suggest a more virulent one. So insistent is West in dramatically and symbolically working out his theme, that only seven[20] of the novel's twenty-seven chapters fail to deal directly with sexual attitudes or experience. Some of them dramatize perversion: the familiar homosexual—there is a homosexual in all of West's novels—in the form of the young female impersonator; but in *The Day of the Locust* he is much more concerned with analyzing masculine impotence and, to a lesser extent, a compensatory lechery.

The note of masculine impotence, though this time not sexual, is established as early as the second chapter, when Abe Kusich has been thrown out of a woman's apartment on " 'Lysol Alley.' " Whether West had a symbolic intention in mind in making Abe a dwarf is unclear. What is clear is that his size is conversely related to his murderous frustration and rage. Dwarfed in stature but not in sexuality—he is, pathetically, a great patron of prostitutes—he alone of the males responds actively, not passively, to Faye's hypnotic sensuality: he fights for her by seizing Earle's testicles until Earle collapses. Moreover, even though he has been beaten brutally, he is the sole male not depressed or made melancholy by the evening's experience. Delighted that he " 'fixed that buckeroo,' " he suggests that they " 'go see some girls. I'm just getting started.' " (p. 140)

Stanley Edgar Hyman has noted that despite West's obsessive sexuality, there are few consummations.[21] It is a penetrating observation; and in no other novel does West take so much delight in frustrating his heroes. But it is a masochistic delight—not at all the sort of glee he took in having Betty Prail raped. Always passive in nature, West's males in *The Day of the Locust* are positively servile. Their frustration is the inevitable consequence of their emasculation.

Predisposed by temperament to make the female the stronger sexual partner in all his novels, West nowhere else develops this motif so elaborately. From the moment Abe Kusich is introduced, on the floor, women dominate the action of the novel. In addition to the slut, there is Mrs. Schwartzen, a stunning abstraction of jaded prurience. One exchange between Tod, Alice Estee—who, one learns, is far from a retiring flower—and Mrs. Schwartzen is particularly illuminating. Mrs. Schwartzen is speaking:

> "Well, I wish we were going to a brothel this minute," she said. "I adore them."
>
> She turned to Tod and fluttered her eyelids.
>
> "Don't you, Mr. Hackett?"
>
> "That's right, Joan darling," Alice answered for him. "Nothing like a bagnio to set a fellow up. Hair of the dog that bit you."
>
> "How dare you insult me!"
>
> She stood up and took Tod's arm.
>
> "Convoy me over there."
>
> She pointed to the group of men with whom Claude was standing.
>
> "For God's sake, convoy her," Alice said. "She thinks they're telling dirty stories." (p. 14)

After the party, the entire group visits Mrs. Jennings, who "ran her business just as other women run lending libraries, shrewdly" (p. 19). A sample: she required "sportsmen" to pass a personal interview before she permitted them to play games.

"Copulation, and death," wrote Eliot; and West must have agreed, for they are both central elements in all his novels. It is therefore to be expected that after Mrs. Jennings, West introduces Mrs. Johnson, "an officious, bustling woman . . . [whose] hobby was funerals":

> There was a knock on the door. Tod answered it and found Mrs. Johnson, the janitress. . . .
>
> "Come back later," Tod said.
>
> He shut the door in her face. A minute later it opened again and Mrs. Johnson entered boldly. She had used a pass-key. (p. 85).

Mary Dove, who is more like a shrike, silences Tod by shouting, "'Go peddle your tripe!'" With Romola Martin (who is, not surprizingly, no match for Homer), she is the third prostitute in the novel; Faye makes a parttime fourth. In a short novel, they total a score slightly better than par for West, and typical of his vision: a prurient woman, an unfaithful wife (Harry's wife is repeatedly unfaithful and finally runs off with a magician), a madame, and three and one-half whores.

It is difficult to decide whether these feminine sexual aberrations are the cause or the result of masculine impotence. Perhaps West saw no simple causal relationship; the novel suggests that he was little interested in determining any such relationship. Instead, he seemed to be concerned with depicting the individual disorder and suggesting its possible larger social consequences.

As in *Miss Lonelyhearts,* West refrains from developing his analysis psychologically; instead, he allows standard Freudian symbols to suggest the neurosis. Sometimes the images are merely casually suggested, as when one of the funeral starers is described as a "man sucking on the handle of a home-made walking stick" (p. 91); or when Claude's involved comic rhetoric about brothels is given an added fillip by the pervasive Freudian *double-entendre,* e.g., "'take a firm grip on your umbrella'" (p. 18). At other times, the psychological images are more fully developed. After seeing Faye at a particularly ravishing moment ("She was much more than pretty. . . . She looked just born, everything moist and fresh, volatile and perfumed"), Tod suddenly "became very conscious of his dull, insensitive feet bound in dead skin and of his hands, sticky and thick, holding a heavy, rough felt hat" (p. 108). The psychological significance of the scene "becomes clear through the symbolic equation of foot and penis,"[22] and of hat and penis. One wonders whether West is suggesting here that Tod suffers from the same itch as Homer.

West's achievement in *The Day of the Locust* lies, however, in his "imagistic" analysis of Homer Simpson, who individually dramatizes not only the disorder but, by his violent attack on Adore, ultimately the behavior of the crowd. West's study of the crowd is thus both particular and general, for in many ways Homer is an extreme portrait of one of those who had "come to California to die." As usual, West has reverted to extremes to make his point—this time, that those who had "come to California to die" had never lived. Homer seems to be aware of this, for he needs sleep but is terrified of it:

> Although it was still early in the afternoon, he felt very sleepy. He was afraid to stretch out and go to sleep. Not because he had bad dreams, but because it was so hard for him to wake again. When he fell asleep, he was always afraid that he would never get up. (p. 31)

It is clear that West is trying to illustrate Homer's deadness and repressed sexuality. West reinforces this suggestion by describing Homer as "a poorly made automaton" and further emphasizes it in the Romola Martin episode.

In Homer, West again presents a classic case study of an Oedipal-induced neurosis which culminates in catatonia.[23] As in Miss Lonelyhearts, the problem is sexual, and it is never made explicit but is immediately developed through imagery. Thus, the first significant remark made about Homer aside from his "fever eyes and unruly hands" is the one noting his fear of sleep.

In view of the fact that sleep disturbance is the most obvious symptom of repressed conflict,[24] West could hardly have chosen a more immediately suggestive image. West probes no further, but on the same page he presents a picture of Homer's hands:

> Every part was awake but his hands. They still slept. He was not surprised. They demanded special attention. . . .
>
> He . . . carried his hands into the bathroom. He turned on the cold water. When the basin was full, he plunged his hands in up to the wrists. They lay quietly on the botton like a pair of strange aquatic animals. When they were thoroughly chilled and began to crawl about, he lifted them out and hid them in a towel. . . . He kept his enormous hands folded quietly on his belly. Although absolutely still, they seemed curbed rather than resting. (p. 31)

West returns again and again to these hands. One cannot fully appreciate their reappearance, however, until he realizes that they are a monstrous symbol of sexual frustration and masturbation. Homer's conflicts, "originally connected with the Oedipus complex," have been "displaced onto the act of masturbation."[25] His hands, then, symbolize a deeply repressed compulsion to masturbate. The following passage reveals how thoroughly complete the repression is:

> He got out of the tub . . . felt even more stupid and washed out than usual. It was always like that. His emotions surged up in an enormous wave, curving and rearing, higher and higher, until it seemed as though the wave must carry everything before it. But the crash never came. Something always happened at the very top of the crest and the wave collapsed to run back like water down a drain. (p. 37)

This description, probably meant to be a clue to the imagery of the hands, is about as close to analysis as West ever comes.

The next time Homer's hands are given attention is during Homer's flashback recollection of the Romola Martin episode. Homer prepares to see her, feeling "almost gay. His step was buoyant and he had completely forgotten his troublesome hands." (p. 34) The sexual anticipation of his meeting provides an outlet in action for his masturbatory inclinations. As Homer cries in his tub over the incident—the *hot* water seems to induce the recollection—one is made to see that this missed opportunity is the only genuine emotional experience he has ever had, the only feeling he has ever felt. The "little waves of sensation" he had felt terrified him because they were strange and new. It was a pleasant sensation and he did not want to lose it:

> Homer was too busy with his growing excitement to speak or even think. He closed his eyes to tend it better, nursing carefully what he felt. He had to be careful, for if he went too fast, it might wither and then he would be cold again. It continued to grow. (p. 35)

But it only lasted a moment, and then it died—stillborn. "It was all over." And "now in California, he was crying because he had never seen Miss Martin again" (p. 36). The masturbatory impulses that found an outlet in the incident with Romola Martin find no such expression when he first meets Faye Greener:

> His hands began to bother him. He rubbed them against the edge of the table to relieve their itch, but it only stimulated them. When he clasped them behind his back the strain became intolerable. They were hot and swollen. Using the dishes as an excuse, he held them under the cold water tap of the sink. (p. 53)

Note that the water is again cold. The next day,

> His hands kept his thoughts busy. They trembled and jerked, as though troubled by dreams. To hold them still, he clasped them together. Their fingers twined like a tangle of thighs in miniature. He snatched them apart and sat on them. (p. 56)

West's comment immediately afterward underlines the point that the violence of Homer's response is but a mark of the violent pressure of his repression:

> When the days passed and he couldn't forget Faye, he began to grow frightened. He somehow knew that his only defense was chastity, that it served him, like the shell of a tortoise, as both spine and armor. He couldn't shed it even in thought. If he did, he would be destroyed.
>
> He was right. (p. 56)

West returns to the image of sleep to communicate Homer's newly aroused state:

> His thoughts frightened him. . . .
>
> In his troubled state . . . he was unable to fall asleep. He closed his eyes and tried to make himself drowsy. . . . Just as he was about to give up, habit came to his rescue. . . .
>
> When he awoke it was without a struggle. He tried to fall asleep once more, but this time couldn't . . . He was thoroughly awake. He tried to think of how very tired he was, but he wasn't tired. (p. 57)

Sexual desires having come to the surface, Homer has difficulty falling asleep; but having emerged somewhat, once asleep he does not have to expend as much energy to suppress them. Hence the more restful sleep.[26]

Later in the novel, however, as Homer becomes less successful at repressing his subconscious wishes, he has trouble sleeping. He wakes unexpectedly to find Mig and Faye in bed. The results are the catatonic withdrawal and the rage that culminates in the riot. Just prior to this discovery, however—after the cock fight and during the party at which Faye's sensual power reduces everyone to quivering desire—West finally reveals Homer's psychogenic masturbatory tic in all its elaborateness:[27]

> His [Homer's] big hands left his lap, where they had been playing "here's the church and here the steeple," and hid in his arm-

> pits. They remained there for a moment, then slid under his thighs. A moment later they were back in his lap. The right hand cracked the joints for the left, one by one, then the left did the same service for the right. They seemed easier for a moment, but not for long. They started "here's the church" again, going through the entire performance and ending with the joint manipulation as before. He started a third time, but catching Tod's eyes, he stopped and trapped his hands between his knees.
>
> It was the most complicated tic Tod had ever seen. (p. 134)

There are, of course, other "pschoanalytic" images: Homer's fear of darkness reflects his "fear of being alone . . . of being overwhelmed by excitation."[28] Such psychoanalytic symbolism permitted West, within a narrative and dramatic context, to study the "crowd" as an individual and a social phenomenon.

When Tod first observed Homer and noted that he was not one of the crowd, he was right: at the time, Homer was not. Though he too was "without hope," and though his anguish was "basic and permanent," he had not yet been betrayed. However, once he finds a dream object in Faye, the parallels between Homer and the crowd increase. Like them his dream object is a grotesque joke, worthless and false; like them he is betrayed by it. Once the dream dies, the only spark of life in "their slack minds and bodies" dies too. The result is the permanent boredom of the crowd or the catatonic stupor of Homer. Smothered just beneath the surface of both is a rage of demoniacal proportions.

In its cumulative power, this individual and general study of the crowd is without parallel in West; from the first deeply suggestive image of "the stare" to the riot at the end, the total effect is that of incredible power. The origin of the danger from the crowd is not that of *A Cool Million:* it is not the danger of misguided idealism, of illusions or Americanism. By 1939, with the entire depression behind him, West was no longer concerned with the danger of American illusions, but with the danger of a people stripped bare of their illusions—the bored, broken, and abused. Yet, West's protest is not economic. The danger is not that of people broken by economic deprivation—his "torch-bearers" were not "tough" or "working class", they were "made up of the lower middle classes" (p. 155)—but of people whipped to fury by the emptiness of their existence.

In his description of the crowd outside Kahn's Persian Palace Theatre, a passage of poetic truth that throbs with anger and compassion, West paints the staggering emptiness of their lives. They are like a silent chorus in a Greek tragedy, writhing in the background. Their "stare" is a mute protest, an accusation, and a commentary on the spiritual vacuum that is modern life. At the end of the novel, when they find voice, it is in blind, ruthless, consuming violence. Like Homer who, once awakened from his sleep of death by Faye, sees the emptiness of his life and lashes out at his tormentor, they erupt. In an incredible riot scene that brings the novel to a shattering close, West makes manifest the "fury," the "awful, anarchic power," that had it in it "to destroy civilization."

Though superficially the result of frustrations originating in stupefying boredom, the riot has a sexual base. Under cover of the riot, spasms of sexuality ripple through the crowd. "An old man, wearing a Panama hat and horn-rimmed glasses" hugs a girl, puts one of his hands inside her dress, and bites her neck (p. 162). Others in the crowd enjoy themselves by relating pervert stories and punning badly on the proper "tool" to use in "ripping up a girl" (p. 164).

Is West suggesting that all frustrations ultimately are sexual ones? Probably not; he has matured since *Balso Snell.* Instead, after the fashion of many moderns, he seems to suggest that socioeconomic disorders will never fail to translate themselves into psychosexual ones, for sexual behavior is the surest index of the health of a society. Thus, the usual delight West took in portraying sexual ineffectuals is not, as in the other novels, treated as a more-or-less important incidental; more than one of the novel's unifying threads, it is the objective correlative of an effete civilization. Tod and Homer are case studies of a mass sexual frustration, and the riot is the eruption of stopped-up sexuality. Just as in *Miss Lonelyhearts,* where suppressed springs of sexuality find outlet in sadistic violence (Miss Lonelyhearts twisting the arm of the "clean old man"), so here, in a riot bordering on sexual hysteria, there is a fusion of sex and violence. It is the fitting climax of all his novels, but especially of *The Day of the Locust.* Whereas in *A Cool Million* sex and violence alternate, in *The Day of the Locust* West pulls the two closer and closer together as the novel unfolds. Just as the cock fight, saturating the air with these passions, culminates in the party, the party, which ends with a brawl and two in bed, is a fitting prelude to the finale of the novel.

In no other novel is West's obsessive sexuality so insistent. Despite the preoccupation with seduction and perversion in various forms in all his novels, only *The Day of the Locust* contains at its heart a revulsion and warning against the power of sex. Moreover, although West is never one to linger over wholesome sexual relations (there is only one in all of West's work, and that is the country interlude in *Miss Lonelyhearts*), West's earlier treatment of sex is not so repellent. Even Miss Lonelyhearts' homosexual impulses arouse pity rather than revulsion. But in its insistence upon the ugliness and degradation of the sexual appetite, from Tod's enslavement and the perversities of "Le Prédicament de Marie" to the lecherous rioters, *The Day of the Locust* is chilling. The hint of impure air that one occasionally breathes in West's other novels is here more than a hint.

Marked by the darkening of his humor—particularly of his sexual humor—there is a deepening of West's pessimism in *The Day of the Locust.* The novel bears a relationship to *Miss Lonelyhearts* much like the relationship between *The Waste Land* and "The Love Song of J. Alfred Prufrock": a bitter, amorphous tragisatire has superseded a dramatic tragicomedy. However, while Eliot often sacrifices the particular for the general and the literal for the symbolical, West roots his novel in reality. Hollywood is not above all the "Unreal City," it is Hollywood—a recognizable Hollywood; Tod is not first of all the artist-prophet, he is Tod; sham is not encountered in the guise of any counterfeit drugstore Indian but in the person of Chief Kiss-My-Towkus. That West has succeeded in realistically dramatizing his vision is suggested by the usual rather realistic reading of the novel.

While this discussion does not attempt to indicate all of the symbolic implications of the novel, not even to develop all of its themes—it merely attempts to point out their dimensions—it does suggest the inadequacy of a reading performed on a rigidly literal and dramatic level. The novel is not a dramatized story; it is a prophecy. And what is its moral? Is it merely that modern man has been emasculated? that violence is displaced love gone wild? that the universal emotional impoverishment of modern man is the consequence of a "jaded palate"? It is hard to say. What emerges clearly from *The Day of the Locust* is not a moral, but a vision of torn, emotion-starved masses whose fury borders on holocaust.

It is this vision that Tod has when, in the midst of the terrifying riot that ends *The Day of the Locust,* he reflects on his picture, "The Burning of Los Angeles":

> Across the top, parallel with the frame, he had drawn the burning city, a great bonfire of architectural styles, ranging from Egyptian to Cape Cod colonial. Through the center, winding from left to right, was a long hill street and down it, spilling into the middle foreground, came the mob carrying baseball bats and torches. For the faces of its members, he was using the innumerable sketches he had made of the people who came to California to die; the cultists of all sorts, economic as well as religious, the wave, airplane, funeral and preview watchers—all those poor devils who can only be stirred by the promise of miracles and then only by violence. (p. 165)

This was West's final statement—and warning: The locusts have descended; the day of the Lord is at hand . . . with death by fire.

VIII. "Westian Man"

THE "reality" West treated in these four small novels is limited but exhaustively analyzed. It is not an objective reality, nor is it unquestionable. Facts are not demanded of an author. What is demanded is the ability to transform a poetic vision into understandable terms. West has succeeded in distilling the essence of Western culture, and he has done so by violently dramatizing a particular image of man, which for convenience has been called "Westian man." It is the reappearance of this peculiarly modern neurotic personality that gives West's novels their coherence. The reader can hardly understand the consistency or character of West's vision without understanding the nature of this unique image; however, one can understand him better by first discussing his opposite.

To speak of West's male type as having an opposite is deceptive. With the exception of a few very minor characters such as Earle Shoop, Miguel, and Abe Kusich, and the more important Homer Simpson, West created no other male type than Westian man. The most glaring exceptions are Shagpoke Whipple and Lem Pitkin in *A Cool Million;* but, as already noted, they are special cases. West, however, has clearly portrayed women differently from men. The differences seem to be so great that one feels a deep sense of the total incompatibility of the sexes.

West never states the matter in such explicit terms, but his treatment of the relationship of the sexes strongly suggests such a pessimistic conclusion. Every Westian man is involved in an unrewarding or frustrating relationship with a female. Light, citing West's contempt for womankind, notes that "Odo of Cluny's reference to the female as a *saccus stercoris* was one of his favorite comments."[1] Even without such evidence, the novels suggest misogynistic tendencies. Only a superficial study of them, however, would lead one to believe that West despised women. Despite his tendency to give them degrading roles, he reveals, at a deeper level, a genuine ambivalence toward them, although he depicts them as uniformly objectionable. With the exception of Mary McGeeney, the prototype of the modern female intellectual, they are almost universally simple-minded. Within this large classification, some are well-meaning and innocent; others are destructive without being themselves destructible. They are, to put it simply, the stronger sex, and stronger because so naïve, stupid, resilient, egocentric, and annoyingly self-sufficient.

Even the Lepi, Janey Davenport, manifests these characteristics. She clearly controls the situation when Balso tries to seduce her:

> Balso took her home and, in the hallway of her house, tried to seduce her. She allowed him one kiss, then broke away. . . .
>
> He made another attempt, but she fended him off. . . ."Tumbling in hallways at my age! How can you? After all, there are the eternal verities, not to speak of the janitor. And besides, we were never properly introduced."
>
> After half an hour's sparring, he managed to warm her up a bit. . . . "If you only loved me, Balso. If you only loved me." He looked her in the eye, stroked her hump, kissed her brow, protesting desperately: "But I do love you Janey. I do. I do. I swear it. I must have you. I must! I must!" She shoved him away with a sad yet determined smile. "First you will have to prove your love as did the knights of old. . . . I want you to kill a man called Beagle Darwin. . . ." (*Balso Snell*, pp. 38-39)

The entire episode is ridiculous; however, her determination and control, while comic, are real. Moreover, there is a hardness in her determination to kill Beagle Darwin. Her letters, of course, reveal her to be naïve and stupid.

The episode is too absurd to be of much argumentative use; but it is worth noting what aspects of social intercourse West chooses to dramatize and render ridiculous. He is laughing at a certain human relationship; nevertheless, his perception of the sordid nature of that relationship comes through the laughter—a perception which changed little with time.

Janey is unpleasant, but no more so than Mary McGeeney,

who, besides being a "middle aged woman dressed in a mannish suit and wearing horn-rimmed glasses," is disturbingly intellectual. She is the first of three Marys who represent the modern woman. That West is here trying to point out the defeminization of overintellectualism is suggested by a heavily ironic passage:

> . . . Balso examined his interrogator with interest. She was a fine figure of a woman.
>
> . . . . .
>
> Balso realized that she was indeed Mary. Changed, alas! but with much of the old Mary left, particularly about the eyes. No longer was she dry and stick-like, but a woman, warmly moist.
>
> They sat and devoured each other with looks until the waiter suggested that they leave as he wanted to close the place and go home.
>
> They left arm-in-arm, walking as in a dream. Balso did the steering and they soon found themselves behind a thick clump of bushes. Miss McGeeney lay down on her back with her hands behind her head and her knees wide apart. . . . (*Ibid.*, pp. 57-58)

What West wanted women to be is unclear; but he did not want them to be intellectual. When they are, they appear ridiculous. When they are the opposite, they are either insipidly wholesome or destructively animalistic: they are, respectively, the Bettys and the Fayes of this world.

The vapidity of the Bettys is terrifying. They have neither dimension nor depth. They are cowlike. In *Miss Lonelyhearts,* Betty's smile is described as "neither 'wry,' 'ironical,' nor 'mysterious'" (p. 28). In the context of the scene, there is only one other kind of smile: wholesome simplicity akin to vacuity. She is described as a "Buddha"; she has the serenity of the simple-minded. West, as well as Miss Lonelyhearts, criticizes her:

> . . . he had once thought that if her world were larger, were *the* world, she might order it as finally as the objects on her dressing table.
>
> . . . . .
>
> [But] her world was not the world. (p. 26-27)

She is, of course, no match for Betty Prail in *A Cool Million.* Betty Prail is so simple that nothing affects her. Rape, white slavery, and streetwalking leave no impression; she is extremely adaptable. She makes the transformation from trollop to tender-hearted innocent in one page (p. 213). Her optimism remains undiminished. At the end of the novel, as Mr. Whipple's secretary, she is still "young and beautiful," and, one might add, innocent and stupid. In this respect she is like Betty "the party dress" in *Miss Lonelyhearts.*

What is interesting about both Bettys, however, is the physical violence they suffer. They are victims of hostility, and yet their responses are incredibly tranquil. Even when Miss Lonelyhearts catches at Betty's nipple, she remains "silent" and makes no sign of noticing. The desire to arouse a response in this "Buddha" results in a show of hostility:

> "Let me pluck this rose," he said, giving a sharp tug. "I want to wear it in my buttonhole."
>
> Betty reached for his brow. "What's the matter?" she asked. "Are you sick?"
>
> He began to shout at her, accompanying his shouts with gestures that were too appropriate, like those of an old-fashioned actor.
>
> "What a kind bitch you are. As soon as any one acts viciously, you say he's sick. Wife-torturers, rapers of small children, according to you they're all sick. No morality, only medicine. . . ." (*Miss Lonelyhearts*, pp. 29-30)

In *A Cool Million,* Betty Prail is subjected to the grossest of humiliations. One cannot help feeling that rape is motivated by a desire to degrade as well as by a desire to achieve sexual satisfaction. It seems too intimately linked with a feeling of hostility, and so calculated to scar, that Betty's psychological virginity is suggestive in more than one sense. Certainly West's delight in the rape of Betty Prail is undisguised, as when he describes her ride with white slavers to "a house of ill fame in New York City":

> The trip was an exceedingly rough one for our heroine. The wagon in which she was conveyed had no springs to speak of, and her two captors made her serve a severe apprenticeship to the profession they planned for her to follow. (*A Cool Million,* p. 167)

At the other extreme are the Fayes. Equally stupid, they are, however, sensual and self-sufficient. From the placid cow one moves to the temptress and tigress. Fay Doyle in *Miss Lonelyhearts* is a crude and incidental portrait of the predatory female: her desires are strong, her behavior direct; there is nothing subtle about her. Her portrait is riddled with clichés; her catlike ability to survive setback is almost as trite as her role of "scorned woman." For all this, she lives as a real character, and her effect on other characters seems real. One does not discern how contrived are the elements of her personality; nor does one question the "reality" of her destructive capacity. She is an example of West's ability to create types that remain individuals.

More important and more subtle than the portrait of Fay Doyle is that of Faye Greener. Less animalistic but more sensuous, she acts as instinctively as Fay Doyle. Indeed, throughout the novel she is described in figurative language suggesting her affinity to nature: she smells like "buckwheat in flower" (*The Day of the Locust,* p. 83); she enjoys the "release that wild flight gives . . . a game bird" (*Ibid.,* p. 65); her beauty is "structural like a tree's" (*Ibid.,* p. 89); and finally, just prior to Tod's dream-rape of her, "she would look like a deer" (*Ibid.,* p. 152). It is not her naturalness, her feline parasitism, and unproductivity, but her stupid whims and logic, her unconscious ability to arouse uncontrollable desire and admiration that are disturbing—her power over men. She can pamper her ego because men are gladly willing to pamper her. The result is masculine degradation before a worthless goddess.

There is something particularly apropos in the following simile; there is also something amusingly frustrating about it:

> Nothing could hurt her. She was like a cork. No matter how rough the sea got, she would go dancing over the same waves that sank iron ships and tore away piers of reinforced concrete. He pictured her riding a tremendous sea. Wave after wave reared its ton on ton of solid water and crashed down only to have her spin gaily away. (*Ibid.,* p. 151)

Faye's insignificance, her resiliency and self-sufficiency, and her shallow immersion in the "sea" are mirrored as clearly as her gaiety before it all. But she is interesting for more reasons than her simple ability to arouse irritation. By creating such an unworthy temptress, West has succeeded in dramatizing a theme he raised in *The Dream Life of Balso Snell:* the falseness of civilization. The entire civilized façade crumples before the reality of Faye Greener's sexual attraction.

That West has chosen a creature like Faye Greener to demonstrate this theme reveals the depth of his pessimism. For Faye Greener is hollow. Behind her beautiful exterior there is neither thought nor logic nor intellectual consistency. Her emotions are simple, her passions elemental and unencumbered by cultural accouterments. She refuses to go to bed with Tod Hackett for uncomplicated reasons: not only is he not attractive, but "she didn't love him and he wouldn't further her career" (*Ibid.*, p. 13).

On the primitive level upon which Faye Greener exists, these are excellent reasons. There is no need to find a reason why she sleeps with Earle Shoop or the Mexican—they appeal to her. To ask why is to ask for civilized criteria. West, had he wished, could not have given satisfactory reasons; to have done so would either have destroyed Faye Greener's "innocent," spontaneous gratification of her desires, or it would, by its very simplicity and unsatisfactoriness, have made her too transparent, deliberate, or unattractive. West would have been guilty of overexplicitness; in any event, the rational would have been unnecessarily introduced where it has no place.

The point West seems to be making is that such basic, nonrational desire exists, and not only does it exist in hollow people such as Faye Greener, it exists in all people. And it is so strong that it strips away the false front of civilization. What engages one's emotions so firmly in this aspect of *The Day of the Locust* is the large element of unpleasant truth about it. West has again objectified a state of mind so forcefully that it repels and angers the reader because it forces him to perceive qualities in himself that he would rather not see. It is not Faye Greener who angers him. It is Tod Hackett, and perhaps less Tod than himself. Like Tod, he feels an "irresistible" desire to break the "smooth surface" of Faye's self-sufficiency, not because there is anything wrong with self-sufficiency, but because it is inhuman and makes him only too aware of his own shortcomings. Ugly qualities—envy and lack of tolerance—are brought to the surface in the reader. One could cite numerous examples of West's ability to induce an unpleasant personal response in his readers. It is one of the things that makes the characters in *Miss Lonelyhearts* and *The Day of the Locust* so powerful and so real.

After the Bettys, the Fayes, and various incidental females, there remains only one other female "type" to discuss in West's novels: the Marys. It is interesting that West should have chosen the name usually associated with virginity and purity. Hardly a coincidence, it is more likely an example of West's scathing irony. Mary McGeeney willingly "spreads" her legs, and Mary Shrike is neurotically preoccupied with her virginity. Mary Dove, a foil and only an incidental character, is a prostitute. Unlike the other two types, who are undisturbed by civilization and who merely follow their uncomplicated paths, the Marys are neurotic. They are, in many respects, forms of the "modern" woman—that is, they fit the misogynist's stereotype of the frigid, dissatisfied, overintellectualized, neurotically repressed, unhappy, affected female. They are thoroughly unattractive and yet, in the novels, they remain objects of desire. West undercuts their desirability by explaining its existence in sour terms. Thus, John Gilson adds the following remark to his stated desire to sleep with Mary McGeeney:

> I need women and because I can't buy or force them, I have to make poems for them. God knows how tired I am of using the insanity of Van Gogh and the adventures of Gauguin as can-openers for the ambitious Count Six-Times. And how sick I am of literary bitches. But they're the only kind that'll have me. . . . (*Balso Snell*, pp. 23-24)

In like fashion, Miss Lonelyhearts turns to Mary Shrike with this thought: "He knew only two women who would tolerate him. He had spoiled his chances with Betty, so it would have to be Mary Shrike." (*Miss Lonelyhearts*, p. 45)

West's pessimistic sense of entrapment is finely illustrated in these passages. If, and it seems probable, West is attempting, in exaggerated form to create modern women—and in some respects they are, for all their exaggeration, the most objectively depicted of his women—pessimism can hardly carry him further. As alternatives they are rather repulsive failures; and if there is no other alternative than these women who reflect the most perverse aspect of civilization, his world view is more terrible than it seems at first glance. Yet, after repeated readings, one begins to develop a feeling for West's women which differs little, surprisingly, from the feeling one has for West's men: they too are maimed souls, betrayed by the barrenness of the contemporary scene. But unlike the men, who react violently to life, the women react more quietly and romantically. In retrospect, there is something pathetic about the universal escapism of West's women. For, with the exception of Betty Prail, who is too naïve to escape, all of West's major female characters are romantics: Janey Davenport still talks about "Love" even as Balso unbuttons his pants; and Mary McGeeney begins her invitation to Balso, "Charge, oh poet, the red-veined flowers. . . ." In *Miss Lonelyhearts*, Mary Shrike's romanticism provokes Miss Lonelyhearts' reflections on dreams; Betty, the "party dress," dreams of a wholesome marriage with Miss Lonelyhearts; and even Fay Doyle is a romantic at heart. The extravagance of her language and of her deception as she literally rapes Miss Lonelyhearts is revealing as well as comic:

> He drew back when she reached for a kiss. She caught his head and kissed him on the mouth. At first it ticked like a watch, then the tick softened and thickened into a heart throb. It beat louder and more rapidly each second, until he thought that it was going to explode and pulled away with a rude jerk.
> "Don't," she begged.
> "Don't what?"
> "Oh, darling, turn out the light." (p. 66)

Faye Greener's romanticism is of the same kind.

The women's romanticism is a response to the barrenness of their lives. West's ambivalence toward women is suggested not only by the failure of society to provide creative outlets for them, but by the failure of the men around them: Fay Doyle is married to a cripple; Betty's marriage to Miss Lonelyhearts is a patent impossibility because of his strong latent homosexuality (one of the reasons for his failure with Fay Doyle); even Mary Shrike is married to a "dead Pan," instead of a live one.

Throughout West's novels one has the feeling that, despite all the whoring, women are still sexually the saner of the two sexes. Significantly, both Fayes despise homosexuals; and Betty's efforts to save Miss Lonelyhearts are genuinely moving. But West is basically unconcerned with women's problems; he either is not interested in analyzing their psychological processes, or is unable to do so. Nor does he appear to create women for their own sake; their importance in his novels lies in their ability to clarify the protagonist's nature. They are, in essence, foils for revelatory purposes. In a sense, West's primary purpose was the creation and revelation of Westian man.

West, himself, was fully aware of the superficial unreality of his characters; they posture and are psychologically paper thin because "Psychology has nothing to do with reality nor should it be used as a motivation. The novelist is no longer a psychologist."[2] The characters do not live and breathe, but they do disturb. They act upon the reader in this way because they strike a chord within him which makes him supply the nuances—nuances drawn from his own psychological makeup. For example, West, in describing his "torchbearers," emphasizes their stare. It is a brilliant find, for in American society, people do not stare. Those who do are . . . whatever they are is supplied by the reader; West does not supply him with details. There is no need to repeat how Tod's responses to Faye are similarly filled in by the reader.

This incompleteness of presentation, along with the subsequent additions of the reader, results in the reader's peculiar ambivalence. The characters are unlovely but nonetheless pathetic; unpleasant and unsympathetic, and yet capable of arousing pity. One has the distinct impression that such a mixed response is due less to West's fusion of feeling and satire than to reader identification. The reader is experiencing an objectified self-pity or self-contempt.

Identification as an aspect of West's art is not an unquestionable hypothesis. However, if one rejects this theory, one finds it hard to explain one's great involvement; it is difficult to remain indifferent to the characters. They are upsetting, and it seems that if they do not arouse the reader's pity, they arouse his anger. In either event, his response seems to be as much the result of his own self-concept as of the objective presentation of character. If one's world view is similar to West's, one's response is probably that of pity muddied by anger; if one's view differs, one may still feel pity, or one may feel anger. Either response is hard to justify textually. The characters are too ambiguous, and one may find passages to support either emotion.

The ambiguity is undoubtedly intentional; it is not only part of

West's world view, it is a reflection of his secretive nature. Such ambiguity cannot be condemned as inartistic, because it is not the result of shoddy craftsmanship but rather of the nature of the portrait. It is one thing to condemn an author for an ambiguous portrait, but another to condemn him because one's own attitude toward the portrait is ambiguous. Both ambiguous portraits and responses are true to life, but the former, unlike the latter, may or may not be related to artistic problems. There is a peculiar power in the latter form of ambiguity: it is the power to arouse thought. This ability to engage the reader's intellect as well as his emotions is characteristically Westian; the reader feels as well as understands the implications of the problem presented. This kind of total involvement of the reader is demanded by most important writers.

It is this ability to breathe life into otherwise unlifelike, often grotesque, characters that makes West so remarkable and so modern. And it is his ability to communicate his own intensity that brings them to life. Nothing strikes the reader more forcefully about West's characters than their intensity. His characters are anguished. A passage from *Miss Lonelyhearts* dramatizes this nervous energy teetering on the brink of violence:

> The cigarette was imperfect and refused to draw. Miss Lonelyhearts took it out of his mouth and stared at it furiously. He fought himself quiet, then lit another one. (p. 5)

It is a classic example. West has chiseled out in fewer than thirty words the major characteristics of Miss Lonelyhearts: his ineffectuality, his intensity, his frustration, and his violence. And he has done it as if in passing, by seizing upon the most banal of human activities. Only great intensity could evoke such a response, and only a good writer could seize upon such a simple image to illustrate it.

More than anything else, it is this disparity between stimulus and response that creates the intensity of Westian man. Such disparity may take the form of incipient violence as it does here; active violence as it does when Miss Lonelyhearts twists the arm of the "clean old man," or when Homer Simpson jumps on Adore's back in *The Day of the Locust*; or verbal hostility as it does more usually. It is not unnatural that West's characters should more often than not express their hostility in the latter fashion; it is West's own mode of aggression, tempered by compassion. His characters are unpleasant largely because of this characteristic. In both instances, the hostility is the result of a painfully frustrating vision, a vision which was so pervasive and intense as to be almost physical. Both West and his characters feel the effects of their vision with the pain of a blow. It is as physically real to them as verbal humiliation is to any sensitive man.

It is this sense of total ego involvement in an unendurable experience that explains his characters' self-consuming anguish. They are not really masochists, although they manifest a great degree of masochism; they are self-annihilators—victims of a death wish. Self-consciousness, however, and an abiding sense of futility—even of such a gesture—as well as a general ineffectuality prevent them from any dramatic, destructive action. In fact, they prevent them from acting in any directed manner at all. Miss Lonelyhearts' friends telling stories in Delehanty's bar are fine examples of this paralysis and slow self-destruction.

In their way, these men are as ineffectual as Miss Lonelyhearts. What renders the ineptness of West's characters so terrible, however, are the incidents by which he dramatizes it. Sometimes the ineffectualness is trivial, as when Miss Lonelyhearts cannot light a cigarette or Tod Hackett find an apartment; and sometimes it is terrible, as in Miss Lonelyhearts' brutally inept slaughter of the lamb. More often than not, however, it is sexual and, for that reason, for West, degrading. Without exception, West's characters are sexually incompetent.

Thus, John Gilson, who writes Dostoevskian journals in hopes of sleeping with Miss McGeeney, fails. Balso Snell fails in his attempted seduction of Janey Davenport, the Lepi; and his ecstatic climax with Mary McGeeney is nothing but a nocturnal emission. Miss Lonelyhearts is comically ineffectual in his efforts to get Mary Shrike to sleep with him; he is almost equally so in his relations with Betty and Fay Doyle. Even Shrike is revealed in one illuminating burst of insight to be pathetically incapable of having his wife when he so desires. Lemuel Pitkin, who is almost a pure study of naïve ineffectualness, probably never goes to bed with Betty Prail, although it certainly cannot be because she is virginal.

Tod Hackett's frustrated passion for Faye Greener is the last and most exhaustive picture of degrading sexual inadequacy.

It is a moot question why West has used sex so often to dramatize his characters' ineffectualness. Certainly it was common enough. Faulkner, Hemingway, and Eliot, to name only a few modern writers, used sex for similar symbolic purposes. And certainly it is a passion basic enough to serve West's purpose; it is vivid enough to capture the right degree of intensity—it is earthy without being sordid; and, being so personal, it is justly calculated to engage the reader in unconscious comparison and thereby to provoke the desired involvement and detachment so characteristic of West's work. West probably selected it, however, because of its universality and its symbolic value. The disorder of the individual mirrors the disorder of the society. Sexual inadequacy is ineffectualness at its most primitive biological level. Tied up in one vivid image are man's social, biological, psychological, and "metaphysical" inadequacies—man's inadequacy before the "laws of life."

For West, sex was such a primary motivating force that it shaped, if it did not determine, most human behavior. At the same time, it was a force as inexplicable as any other one might choose, and also one which concretely dramatized forces beyond man's control. In *Miss Lonelyhearts,* and more particularly in *The Day of the Locust,* West has crystallized man's helplessness before unknown forces; and he has done it without becoming immersed in the age-old controversy of free will and determinism, without imprinting the wooden stamp of determinism on his characters. Perhaps it is his feeling of impotence, of being swept up by incompletely understood forces, that contributes to the passivity of Westian man. He is not an actor, not even active or directed enough to be a reactor; he is a person to whom things happen—a victim.

It is not strange, therefore, that West's characters are frustrated. West's brilliance, however, proceeds from his ability to generalize frustration. One never has the impression that the frustration is merely sexual. Even in *The Day of the Locust,* where sexual frustration is almost a leitmotif, one does not have the feeling that Faye Greener's capitulation to Tod will change anything. The sexual frustration is merely a symbol of a more permanent and more pervasive ailment.

Even after the savage iteration of this theme, the theme of spiritual frustration still fixes itself in one's mind. It was the inevitable consequence not only of West's archetypal and sociological intention but of his ability to communicate his idealism through his characters. Degraded, abused, violent, pathetic souls, they are nonetheless aspiring ones. So important and redeeming an aspect of West's characters is aspiration that one is tempted to say that it is only the lack of it in Shrike which makes him such an ugly character and which sets him apart from the rest of West's major characters. Perhaps this cynicism more than any other characteristic contributes to one's especial lack of sympathy for him; and perhaps the lack of this humanizing quality explains his destructive pursuit of Miss Lonelyhearts. He is a terrifying portrait because he believes in nothing; he has been cheated, and in the violence of his reaction to this realization, he has lost compassion. He is, in many respects, an individualized study of those who "came to California to die" in *The Day of the Locust,* except that he has more power, courage, and direction.

The other characters are different in kind. They too feel cheated; they too are often destructive. Yet, they still have aspirations—delusionary perhaps, but aspirations which help to temper their sadism, which help to divert their energies from destructiveness, but which at the same time make their frustration almost unbearably intense. Unlike Shrike, they have not been able to dress their frustration in nihilistic armor, they have not learned to handle their frustrations intellectually; and so they merely suffer. Unlike Shrike—who almost convinces one that he does not suffer—their anguish is extreme and permanent.

Unfortunately, aspirations have a tendency to ennoble people—often unduly. West did not want such ennoblement; at least, he never permitted aspiration to have this effect. By selecting goals which are degrading or unattainable, and by making the pursuit of these goals absurd and comical, he has emphasized his characters'—and man's—insignificance; and he has largely done it by focusing on inadequacies of character as well as on defects in society. By placing the blame for man's spiritual starvation on self as well as on society, West has prevented his reader from wholeheartedly sympathizing with his characters' plight, and, as a consequence, to a lesser extent with his own. West forces him to see man's essential unloveliness. Thus, with the exception of Miss Lonelyhearts, there is not one character in West's novels who can be said to have exalted aims; and even Miss Lonelyhearts' noble aim is tarnished by his lack of dignity and his disturbed emotional state.

There are numerous examples of debased goals in West's novels: Maloney the Areopagite's goal is to cannonize a flea, John Gilson's goal is to seduce Miss McGeeney, Beagle Darwin's is to create striking effects, Shrike's is to torture Miss Lonelyhearts, and Tod Hackett's is to sleep with Faye Greener. There is not one —not even Lemuel Pitkin's or Homer Simpson's—that is not made to seem ugly or basically ridiculous. When the goal itself is not unpleasant, the character who pursues it is so pathetic or comic in his pursuit that one ignores, if one even realizes, the worth of the goal; even more fitting in West's scheme of things, one recognizes the impossibility of attaining the goal. The result is always the same: whether the goals are worthless or whether unattainable, a sense of entrapment is communicated.

For West, entrapment was a fundamental issue: man is trapped, and any pretension at being otherwise leads to tragic frustration and destruction. Yet man's very nature seems to demand ideals, for in West's world, man seems to be unable to exist without dreams. When these dreams are thwarted, as they inevitably are, the result is the boredom of those who "came to California to die"; the violence of Shrike, Miss Lonelyhearts, Homer, and the crowd in *The Day of the Locust*; or the insanity of Miss Lonelyhearts. For West, man's lot is a miserable one, and only ignorance of that fate can permit one to go on; West makes it clear, however, that he has no sympathy with such ignorance.

That West does not share it and does not want others to be able to is evidenced not only by his created world but by the people who populate it. With the exception of Homer Simpson, their misery is not that of a wounded animal, suffering without an awareness of its source and deserving of being put out of his misery; it is a fully self-conscious suffering. They are only too aware of life and thus rendered more sensitive to its pains.

It is this self-consciousness of existence and this awareness of what life, as West saw it, really means that increases their sense of entrapment[3] and their frustration, two obvious symptoms of the neurotic syndrome. And, in fact, they are textbook neurotics. They have that peculiar repellent yet pathetic defensiveness. Confronted with the impossible alternatives of ignorance or anguish, it was perhaps inevitable that they should be given to posturing in an attempt to suppress knowledge of their dilemma. The purpose of the suppression like their self-mockery, is self-defense. By laughing at themselves, they hope to disengage themselves from a painful perception.

There is, in the sum total of their responses, a strangely hunted quality. In West's work, the distinction between the feverish quester and the wracked scapegoat is an infinitely fine or nonexistent one. West's peculiar gift was his ability to haunt his quester, who conveys the gaunt desperation of the pursued in flight.

In the desperation with which they pursue their ugly defenses, they arouse those true cathartic emotions of pity and terror. For despite their suffering, the natural culmination of their inadequate defenses, of their neuroses, is an intensity bordering on violence. And this violence, whose prodrome is boredom and whose symptom is frustration, will erupt because its purpose is self-preservation, because it is the product of great suffering and its only means of release.

Perhaps, ultimately, what makes West's work so unpleasant and upsetting is this ability to generalize an image of man as a diseased, endlessly suffering victim. For some, there is something vaguely indecent and terrifying about such an image, about exposing such suffering. William Carlos Williams, a close friend of West's, inadvertently summed it up as well as it probably ever will be: "Should such lives," he asked, "as these letters [in *Miss Lonelyhearts*] reveal never have been brought to light? Should such people, like the worst of our war wounded, best be kept in hiding?"[4] For many readers the answer is "yes"; for them, the "private masochistic alchemy by which West tried to erase the vision of suffering humanity he saw around him"[5] results in a work of art with, to paraphrase Wordsworth, a greater proportion of pain than may be endured. Most, however, feel differently, and therein lies a hint of the dimension of West's achievement; for only a very fine writer could have transcended such a vision of unrelieved, unbearable human suffering.

IX. "He Charts Our World"

WEST's originality and modernity are only now beginning to be appreciated. It is difficult to understand why previous readers lagged in this respect. Perhaps his small output, a too realistic reading by his readers, and his melancholy insistence on suffering and defeat all militated against him. Moreover, though there is much ingenuity in West's novels, ultimately there is little variety. He did not have great range. Troubled by a vision of a civilization going under, he sounded but one note, and that a half-warning, half-despairing cry.

In his two masterpieces, West, like many another modern artist, sought out a mythic lens through which to view his age and to compare its contemporary distortions against a backdrop of eternity. Viewed from such a mythic distance, the aberrations of the time are grotesque; but they are recognizable.

The victim of this age is Westian man, distillation of the modern malaise. A psychological abstraction exaggerated beyond reality, Westian man is nevertheless a powerful, suggestive, and disturbing character. He seems to be an objectification of each reader at his most unsympathetic and pathetic moments. Perhaps much of the hostility directed at him is a defense against the faintly sickening self-pity he arouses.

An archetypal neurotic, Westian man is more complex than he appears. Much of his complexity, as well as that of the novels, is the result of West's method, a fusion of Baudelaire's and Freud's. From Baudelaire West probably derived his belief in the autonomy of the imagination:

> For Baudelaire, the work of art is essentially a work of the imagination and yet it is true and real at the same time. This is perhaps the best way of defining what is meant by the sincerity of a

> work of art: the fidelity with which it adheres to the imagination of the artist. Additionally, for Baudelaire, a work of the imagination comes from a very real kind of anguish. Not so much the impermanent and transitory anguish of daily living, of insecurity, of war and love, as the inner and deeply permanent anguish of man which is usually repressed and covered over with willful forgetfulness. As in the treatment of psychoanalysis, the poet has to go very far down into his past, into the significance of his childhood. . . . Baudelaire's self-discovery in his anguish and his self-revelation in his writing were archetypal. . . . All literature is to some degree psychoanalytic. Baudelaire went so deeply into psychoanalytic exploration that he passed beyond personal reminiscence into the universal.[1]

From Freud West borrowed his myths and many of his symbols. Beneath West's novels there is a Freudian psychoanalytic vein that cannot be ignored. West's use of this symbolic vein is something new and startling in American literature. By using simple images and symbols to suggest the psychological state of his characters, West in his two major works transcends the limits set by their dated references applicable to the American thirties. It is this added psychological dimension that makes Miss Lonelyhearts such an unforgettable character. To a large extent, it is what makes the characters so enormously suggestive and what makes them seem to speak so intimately to the reader. The characters are not deep, but they are vivid; like Sophocles' personages, they seem to burn themselves indelibly into one's mind. Ultimately, it is this psychological method that allows such broad generalization about the characters. They are, to paraphrase West, case studies raised to a mythic level.

The author's interest in Westian man, however, is not merely personal or psychological; it is sociological. In this sociological concern, West bridges the gap between the literature of sensibility, wherein the writer turns inward upon himself in order to unfold his own malaise, and the literature of naturalistic social protest, in which the artist unfolds the working of the society upon the individual. West must have sensed, quite clearly, that his personal estrangement was shared by the society at large, for despite the subjective nature of his inspiration, he suggests the collective tragedy.

West brings home the full horror of his characters' tragedy by assigning these perverted souls religious, mythic roles. Miss Lonelyhearts playing Christ or Percival cuts a comic and pathetic figure; and Tod, musing on a fancied rape of Faye Greener, or shouting "at her like a Y.M.C.A. lecturer on sex hygiene" (*The Day of the Locust,* p. 90), is an inept Jeremiah. The calculated incongruity is grotesquely comic, but there is genuine despair in it as well.

Miss Lonelyhearts and Tod, indeed Westian man, are peculiarly modern figures in their introspection, their schizoid temperament. They represent the new hero, "the unadaptable man, the wanderer or the dreamer or the perpetrator of illogical action."[2] In creating this type, West has not only translated the traditional great myths —the quest, the scapegoat, and the holy fool—into present-day forms, he has exploited some of the newer "pervasive myths or patterns of symbolic statement . . . in contemporary literature . . . the Myth of the Isolato, the Myth of Hell, the Myth of Voyage, and the Myth of Sanctity."[3] These myths are played out on the streets of the city, that most recurrent of modern symbols, which in West and so many other modern novelists is "an image of despair, as it is in Isaiah and Jeremiah."[4]

The mythic conception is obscured by the novels' garish landscapes. The very gift which allowed West to seize upon stark, vivid images worked against him by masking the subsurface meaning. The narrative logic and grotesque texture of his two masterpieces convey their own limited reality. He had a poet's eye and a sociologist's understanding; and whether he was dramatizing Miss Lonelyhearts' searing conflict, or merely satirizing American funeral customs, the density of his created world is sufficient to hold his reader's attention. But West's world was always a half-world; his desire was imaginatively to seize upon a deeper reality. Like so many other modern writers, he "often felt it necessary to use violence and melodrama as instruments for awakening his age out of its lethargies, for destroying its specious securities and revealing its underlying nightmare and tragedy."[5]

Perhaps it is the very violence of his novels, their stridency, and their brilliance which have resulted in so widespread a realistic reading of his work. West's world will never come alive as it should under such a reading. If *Miss Lonelyhearts* is ever to be staged again, it must never be played realistically; it must be played in the new style of Genet, Pinter, and Albee—the style of the absurd.

This is not to represent West as merely a novelist of the absurd; he is more than that. But his work contains elements of the absurd; just how many can be seen by some passages from an essay on Edward Albee. They describe West so well one would think he was a dramatist of the fifties and sixties rather than a novelist of the thirties:

> Both the American and English rebels were in sympathy with those dramatists in Paris (Beckett, Ionesco, Genet) who found that the world, bereft of confidence in traditional values, no longer made sense, was in fact "absurd." Language and ideologies were a currency with nothing in the bank! Substance had dissolved; everything was in fission. Even tragedy was unreal. Despair took on the airs of farce. As Saul Bellow put it, "Things had gotten all mixed up somewhere between laughter and insanity."
>
> These . . . trends . . . struck many observers as nihilistic if not nuts. But it has become increasingly evident that most of the dramatists who wrote these plays were deeply troubled and that what impelled them was not sport or jest but protest. To be sure it was not protest with a program or a "solution" (they no longer knew where to seek one); their plays were jeers, imprecations, outcries of agony—frequently masked as ribald jokes.[6]

Although these remarks do not sum up West, they are suggestive. Ultimately, West's strength is that he is too unique to be classifiable; and perhaps this strength has been, paradoxically, the reason why even now he has failed to capture the critical imagination. It is difficult to find the perspective (realistic? mythic? psychoanalytic?) by which to approach his novels. The works are prismatic, and perspective is important. We are beginning to have that perspective. For West, like Lawrence,

> has made it possible for those who read him critically to understand aesthetically, to grasp in the mode of immediate apprehension aspects of our contemporary world that, had he left them uninformed, would have remained for us mere threatening, oppressive chaos. He charts our world. Without him and the other poets who also chart it, we would be likely to be blind to the specific process of disintegration of which we are victims.[7]

West was one of those rare American phenomena, a visionary, and *Miss Lonelyhearts* and *The Day of the Locust* are his visionary nightmares. They appeal to the deepest wellsprings of man's being, calling up hidden, nameless terrors. They exist in a nightmare world of unreality, and when the reader has left the fictional nightmare, he experiences, as he does in life, that afterglow, that twilight panic and dawning relief which beset the spirit. In West, however, the afterglow is an enduring one.

It may be argued that four short novels, only two of which are likely to endure, do not make a great impression on the literary scene. But if the ability to scar a reader, to leave an indelible impression on a reader's mind, is a mark of achievement, West left that mark the way few other writers do. It is a narrow scar, but a very deep one.

Notes to Chapters

I. INTRODUCTION

1. Alan Ross, Introduction to *The Complete Works of Nathanael West* (New York: Farrar, Straus and Cudahy, 1957), p. xxii.
2. Richard B. Gehman, Introduction to *The Day of the Locust* (New York: New Directions, 1939), p. xxiii.
3. "*Life is terrible,* that was the despairing conclusion that led nowhere and which was the motive spring for his novels. For West there was no religious redemption to be found in human weakness, no transfiguring sense of good-and-evil, no compensation in the physical life. Seediness, apathy remained just seediness and apathy. The joke was on civilization. . . ." (Ross, p. xi)
4. Wallace Fowlie, *Age of Surrealism* (Bloomington: Indiana University Press, 1950), p. 43.
5. *Ibid.*, p. 188.
6. *Loc. cit.*
7. Marc L. Ratner, "'Anywhere Out of This World': Baudelaire and Nathanael West," *American Literature,* XXXI, No. 4 (Jan., 1960), pp. 456-63. As symbolist features Mr. Ratner lists stylistic economy, concentrated incidents which reveal psychological states, use of poetic imagery to achieve a concentrated effect, and finally, a fiction characterized by a "terse epigrammatic style, poetic imagery, and satiric content." (p. 457)
8. Fowlie, p. 188.

II. THE AUTHOR REVEALS HIMSELF

1. James F. Light in his book on West, *Nathanael West: An Interpretive Study* (Evanston: Northwestern University Press, 1961), indicates repeatedly West's admiration for Flaubert. See pages 8, 28, 31, 40. The possible influence of Flaubert on West is a study in itself. Unless explicitly indicated, all further references to Light are to this study.
2. Nathanael West, *The Dream Life of Balso Snell* in *The Complete Works of Nathanael West* (New York: Farrar, Straus and Cudahy, 1957), p. 16. Future references to this work will be incorporated into the text in the following manner: (*Balso Snell,* p. 16) or simply (p. 16). All references and page numbers cite this edition.

3. For want of a better name, and for purposes of simplification, in the future this collective portrait shall be referred to as "Westian man," even though the label is a bit pretentious.

4. Nathanael West, "Some Notes on Miss L.," *Contempo*, Vol. III, No. 9 (May 15, 1933), p. 2.

5. Light, pp. 135-36.

6. West originally had planned to give Miss Lonelyhearts' name as Thomas Matlock, a name which clearly suggests "wrestler with doubts."

7. Richard B. Gehman, Introduction to *The Day of the Locust* (New York: New Directions, 1939), p. x.

8. Nathanael West. Cited by Robert M. Coates, Introduction to *Miss Lonelyhearts* (New York: New Directions, 1933), p. xi.

9. Nathanael West, *Miss Lonelyhearts* (New York: New Directions, 1933), p. 27. Future references to this work will be incorporated into the text in the following manner: (*Miss Lonelyhearts*, p. 27) or simply (p. 27). All references and page numbers cite this edition. These page numbers do not correspond with those in the New Directions paperback, *Miss Lonelyhearts* and *The Day of the Locust.*

10. Light quotes Jack Sanford to this effect. See p. 63.

11. Light, p. 151.

12. Richard McLaughlin, "West of Hollywood," *Theatre Arts*, XXXV (August, 1951), p. 46.

13. Light observes much the same attitude: "Miss Lonelyhearts' desire to identify himself with suffering humanity . . . was quite possibly also an emotion of the creator of *Miss Lonelyhearts.*" (p. 113)

14. Norman Podhoretz, "A Particular Kind of Joking," *New Yorker*, XXXIII (May 18, 1957), p. 165.

15. See Light, p. 30 for a more detailed discussion of the essay.

16. Jack Sanford's remark is quoted by Light. See Light, p. 63.

17. See Light for a detailed discussion of West's attitude toward his Jewishness and Jews in general.

18. Light quotes Philip Lukin to the effect that West "was a dandy when it came to clothes and one would assume that this was an attempt to compensate for his lack of other [attractive] physical attributes." See Light, p. 9.

19. Nathanael West, *The Day of the Locust* (New York: New Directions, 1939), p. 43. Future references to this work will be incorporated into the text in the following manner: (*The Day of the Locust*, p. 43) or simply (p. 43). All references cite this edition. These page numbers also correspond with page numbers in the New Directions paperback containing *Miss Lonelyhearts* and *The Day of the Locust.*

20. West refers to his "particular kind of joking" in a 1939 letter to George Milburn. See Gehman, p. xxii.

21. Wallace Fowlie, *Age of Surrealism* (Bloomington: Indiana University Press, 1950), p. 100.

22. The portrait that emerges in Light's book has a definite serious cast to it.

23. Too much has been made of West's indebtedness to S. J. Perelman in this work. The debt is clear, but there is much to be said for a belief in West's reversion to the earlier attitude and method, a reversion which is understandable when one considers West's humanitarian bent and when one realizes the immediacy with which he felt the problem. Unlike the more philosophical and psychological problems of *Miss Lonelyhearts* and *The Day of the Locust*—problems which for West were part of an unchanging order—the problem of *A Cool Million* is capable of being imminently dangerous. A good case can be made for the supposition that West, knowing the surprise potential of the work, and being emotionally committed to a matter of great *practical* importance without being sure of the accuracy of his vision, reverted to his natural posture of ludicrous defensive exaggeration.

24. Light mentions "a deeper sense of detachment from the world" during his years at the Hotel Sutton. See p. 66.

25. Light quotes Nathan Asch to the effect that beneath West's ironic, sophisticated front there was "a mentality that was tender and an eye that saw true." See p. 73.

III. A STUDY IN TENSION

1. Richard B. Gehman, Introduction to *The Day of the Locust* (New York: New Directions, 1939), pp. xiv-xv. The above passage, and West's general posture, lead one to ask whether West was familiar with Baudelaire's definition of the modern artist as a "dandy." Wallace Fowlie in *Age of Surrealism* (Bloomington: Indiana University Press, 1950), p. 37, notes that *le dandy*, "according to Baudelaire, has critical intelligence and a finely developed sensitivity and character, but he is constantly aspiring to a coldness of feeling, a hardness of character, an insensibility and inscrutability. This is a tight-fitting mask which he must forge every day in order not to betray himself when in the world. The dandy learns how to feign hostility and indifference until they become naturally instinctive to him. His fear is . . . that to appear sincere . . . would be equivalent to appearing ridiculous."

2. Nathanael West, "Some Notes on Miss L.," *Contempo*, Vol. III, No. 9 (May 15, 1933), p. 1.

3. A European rather than American tendency. Thus Kafka's *The Trial*, to cite an illustration, may be read as a symbolic recreation of a

totalitarian experience, a recreation of the experiences of a schizophrenic as viewed by a schizophrenic, and/or a symbolic vision of man's fate.

4. Idris Parry, "Kafka, Gogol, and Nathanael West," in *Kafka: A Collection of Critical Essays*, ed. by Ronald Gray (Englewood Cliffs, N. J.: Prentice-Hall, Inc., 1962), p. 86.

5. Gehman reports West's reply to the assertion by Clifton Fadiman that West was a surrealist: "'He [Fadiman] knows enough about Surrealism, I am sure, to know that I am not a Surrealist at all.'" See p. x.

6. Fowlie, p. 17.

7. *Ibid.*, p. 40.

8. *Ibid.*, p. 41.

9. Gehman, p. 11. Most important for West is degeneracy. The sexual theme runs throughout his novels, particularly in *Miss Lonelyhearts* and *The Day of the Locust.* The decay and disintegration West is concerned with, however, is not physical but moral, spiritual, and social. In this respect, they exist in all his novels. The physical disintegration of Lemuel Pitkin is an exception, and a rare externalization.

10. *Loc. cit.*

11. "Some Notes on Miss L.," p. 1.

12. Nathanael West, "Some Notes on Violence," *Contact*, Vol. I, No. 3 (Oct., 1932), pp. 132-133.

13. "Some Notes on Miss L.," p. 1.

14. Light quotes this description of West by Nathan Asch, an acquaintance of West. James F. Light, *Nathanael West: An Interpretive Study* (Evanston: Northwestern University Press, 1961), p. 73.

15. Cited by Light. *Ibid.*, p. 67.

16. William Carlos Williams, "Sordid? Good God," *Contempo*, Vol. III, No. 11 (July 25, 1933), p. 8.

17. Cited by F. O. Matthiessen, *The Achievement of T. S. Eliot* (New York: Oxford University Press, 1958), p. 89.

IV. THE DREAM LIFE OF BALSO SNELL

1. Richard B. Gehman in the Introduction to *The Day of the Locust* (New York: New Directions, 1939), p. xv, suggests that most of *Balso Snell*, despite its publication in 1931, was completed by the time West returned to the United States in 1926.

2. Among the French writers who influenced West, the following ones are specifically satirized or alluded to in *Balso Snell:* Baudelaire, Rimbaud, Mallarmé, Huysmans, and Gide.

3. James F. Light, *Nathanael West: An Interpretive Study* (Evanston: Northwestern University Press, 1961), p. 54.

4. *Ibid.*, p. 55.

5. Light discusses West's relation to Joyce at length. Several of his remarks are worth repeating here: "West satirized what he felt was Joyce's artistic pretentiousness. . . . West detested falsity, Joycean or otherwise, and therefore despised the phoniness of the inhabitants of the Trojan Horse." (p. 55) ". . . West reflects the influence of that great artist. The form of *Ulysses*, a journey through chaos, makes the form of *Balso* what it is. Even more, the dominant ideas of *Ulysses*, the quest for truth (or the father) and the rejection of false gods, are the central concepts of *Balso*; and West accepts the idea, if not the prose, of Joyce's 'yes' to the body." (p. 56) "I. J. Kapstein calls the *Walpurgisnacht* scene 'the major influence of *The Dream Life*.'" (p. 41)

6. See Light, p. 38.

7. Gehman, p. xv.

8. Alan Ross, Introduction to *The Complete Works of Nathanael West* (New York: Farrar, Straus and Cudahy, 1957), p. xii.

9. Malcolm Cowley, Introduction to *Miss Lonelyhearts* (New York: Avon Book Division, the Hearst Corp., 1959), p. iii.

10. Light, p. 60.

11. "Above all, however, Balso is a rejection of the artistic, the rational, and the spiritual pretensions of man." See Light, p. 41.

12. Many of the themes were probably derived from Arthur Machen's *The Hill of Dreams*. Light cites as its theme "the artist's loneliness, solitude, and separation from mankind." He also indicates that West read Machen "most closely." The overtones of fakery and phoniness inherent in the theme must have appealed to West. See Light p. 27.

13. *Ibid.*, p. 59.

14. Ross, p. xi.

15. *Loc. cit.*

16. Light wisely notes that "one can hardly overlook the sexual implications of the murder." See Light, p. 46.

17. One wonders whether all these experiments were not invaluable to West; they may have been instrumental in perfecting his ability to mimic various styles—an ability which is called into play in the letters in *Miss Lonelyhearts*.

18. Balso's very initials, B. S., seem to be part of the sustained literary joke. West suggests the *double-entendre* of the initials in the lines: "The world was getting to be a difficult place for a lyric poet. He felt old. 'Ah youth!' he sighed elaborately. Ah Balso Snell!'" (pp.

22-23) For West it must have seemed appropriate that *the* poet and dreamer *par excellence* should be given initials suggesting the scatological, anti-intellectual label that summed up for him art, dreams, and perhaps life itself.

19. Light, p. 77.

V. MISS LONELYHEARTS

1. Stanley Edgar Hyman, *Nathanael West* (University of Minnesota Pamphlets on American Writers, No. 21, 1962), p. 27.

2. James F. Light, in *Nathanael West: An Interpretive Study* (Evanston: Northwestern University Press, 1961), notes that after *The Day of the Locust* West "planned to write simple, warm, and kindly books" (p. 182). The remark, of course, may have been mere legpull. In any event, West probably could not have written such books.

3. Francis Fergusson, *The Idea of a Theater: A Study of Ten Plays* (New York: Doubleday Anchor Books, 1957), p. 31.

4. Had West written a conventional tragedy, and had he intended the "mystical union with God" to be ontologically valid, West would have been faced with the question: Is a Christian tragedy possible? But since West had about "as much faith as an ear of corn" (Light quotes Jack Sanford to this effect; see p. 132), the problem never arose.

5. William Flint Thrall, Addison Hibbard, and C. Hugh Holman in *A Handbook to Literature* (New York: The Odyssey Press, 1960) have the following to say about comedy: "In general the comic effect arises from a recognition of some incongruity of speech, action, or character revelation. . . . Comedy itself varies according to the attitude of the author or recipient, tending, where it becomes judicial, toward satire; where it becomes sympathetic, toward pathos and tragedy." (p. 96)

6. James F. Light, "Violence, Dreams, and Dostoevsky: The Art of Nathanael West," *College English*, XXX, pp. 208-09.

7. Light, pp. 86-87.

8. Nathanael West, "Some Notes on Miss L.," *Contempo*, Vol. III, No. 9 (May 15, 1933), p. 2.

9. Light notes that West had read Nietzsche and suggests a "receptivity to Nietzschean ideas" in West. See pp. 30-31. Nietzsche is also included in the grand gallery of influences in *Balso Snell*.

10. Light, pp. 127-28.

11. Hyman, pp. 23-24.

12. Claire Rosenfield, "An Archetypal Analysis of Conrad's *Nostromo,*" The University of Texas *Studies in Literature and Languages,* Vol. III, No. 4 (Winter, 1962), p. 521.

13. Jesse L. Weston, *From Ritual to Romance* (New York: Macmillan Co., 1920).

14. *Ibid.,* p. 12.

15. *Ibid.,* p. 114.

16. *Ibid.,* p. 53.

17. *Ibid.,* p. 52.

18. *Ibid.,* p. 104.

19. *Loc. cit.*

20. *Ibid.,* p. 81.

21. *Ibid.,* p. 80.

22. *Ibid.,* p. 170.

23. *Ibid.,* p. 172.

24. *Ibid.,* p. 119.

25. Joseph Campbell, *The Hero With a Thousand Faces* (Pantheon Books: Bollingen Series XVII, 1949), p. 387.

26. *Ibid.,* p. 180.

27. *Ibid.,* p. 36. Miss Lonelyhearts' death immediately after "The Ultimate Boon" is extremely important, for as Campbell notes: "The *return and reintegration with society,* which is indispensable to the continuous circulation of spiritual energy into the world, and which, from the standpoint of the community, is the justification of the long retreat, the hero himself may find the most difficult requirement of all."

28. *Ibid.,* p. 246.

29. *Ibid.,* p. 81.

30. *Ibid.,* p. 29.

31. *Ibid.,* p. 101.

32. "Some Notes on Miss L.," p. 2.

33. Campbell, p. 102.

34. *Ibid.,* p. 123.

35. *Ibid.,* p. 147.

36. *Ibid.,* p. 59.

37. *Ibid.,* p. 257.

38. "Some Notes on Miss L.," p. 2.

39. Otto Fenichel, M.D., in his book, *The Psychoanalytic Theory of Neurosis* (New York: W. W. Norton and Co., Inc., 1945) finds the "equation *knife = penis* and *cutting = coitus*" to be a fairly standard one in dreams (p. 223). Some further comments on homosexuality are revealing: "Homosexuality has proved to be the product of specific mechanisms of defense, which facilitate the persistence of the re-

pression of both the Oedipus and the castration complex. At the same time, the aim of homosexual object choice is the avoidance of emotions around the castration complex, which otherwise would disturb the sexual pleasure, or at least the attainment of reassurances against them" (p. 341).

40. Fenichel notes: "Many schizophrenics are full of ideas of saving mankind, projections of their awareness that they themselves are in need of salvation" (p. 436). Also: "Catatonic attitudes seem to aim less at regaining objects than at denial of unpleasant feelings or of awareness of sickness. It is as if many catatonic mimetic expressions unsuccessfully intend to say: 'You see I am not insane!' " (p. 439) Note the relevancy of the second comment to Homer in *The Day of the Locust.*

41. Barbara Seward, *The Symbolic Rose* (New York: Columbia University Press, 1960), p. 3.

42. *Ibid.*, p. 7. "In Freudian belief . . . blossoms and flowers in general are said to represent the female sexual organs, while the particular shape of the rose associates it most directly with the shape of the vulva. In other words, to Freud the rose of spring is first and foremost the rose of sexual love."

43. Hyman, p. 22.

44. *Ibid.*, p. 23.

45. Alan Ross, Introduction to *The Complete Works of Nathanael West* (New York: Farrar, Straus and Cudahy, 1957), p. xi.

46. Light, p. 72.

47. Hyman carefully notes in his essay, as I should like to here, that "the pattern of Miss Lonelyhearts' Oedipus complex . . . is not that of West." See Hyman, p. 24.

VI. A COOL MILLION

1. Nathanael West, *A Cool Million* in *The Complete Works of Nathanael West* (New York: Farrar, Straus and Cudahy, 1957), p. 244. Future references to this work will be incorporated into the text in the following manner: (*A Cool Million*, p. 244) or simply (p. 244). All references and page numbers refer to this edition.

2. Alan Ross, Introduction to *The Complete Works of Nathanael West* (Farrar, Straus and Cudahy, 1957), p. xviii.

3. *Ibid.*, p. xvii.

4. Leslie Fiedler in *The American Scholar*, XXV (Autumn, 1956), p. 478, considers but finally rejects *A Cool Million* for the title of "most undeservedly neglected book."

VII. THE DAY OF THE LOCUST

1. Stanley Edgar Hyman, *Nathanael West* (University of Minnesota Pamphlets on American Writers, No. 21, 1962), p. 33 suggests that "Tod never quite comes to life . . . because of West's efforts to keep him from being autobiographical."

2. *Ibid.*, p. 45.

3. Miss Lonelyhearts is a commentator as well. But his comments are fundamentally self-revelatory. Moreover, they seem to grow out of the situation; they are functional, not decorative.

4. Richard B. Gehman, Introduction to *The Day of the Locust* (New York: New Directions, 1939), p. xix.

5. Alan Ross, Introduction to *The Complete Works of Nathanael West* (New York: Farrar, Straus and Cudahy, 1957), p. xi.

6. T. S. Eliot, *The Waste Land,* III. "The Fire Sermon." See Eliot's note to line 218.

7. *Loc. cit.* Eliot remarks that what Tiresias *sees* is the substance of the poem.

8. Here, as in *Miss Lonelyhearts,* West devotes entire chapters to revealing a single relationship. Each chapter thus becomes a unit in itself. Thus, in *The Day of the Locust,* Chapter 1 is devoted to Tod and Hollywood (the masquerades and those who "came to California to die"); Chapter 2, to his relationship with Abe Kusich; Chapter 3, to his relationship with Faye; Chapter 4, to his relationship with Claude Estee; Chapter 6, to his relationship with Harry Greener; etc. At the end, as in *Miss Lonelyhearts,* West brings together all his characters.

9. Note the stylistic device, "but not from . . ."; it is a recurrent pattern used to raise the reader to a pitch, for instead of dropping the tension as it seems to, the phrase increases it. One more example: "She was supposed to look drunk and she did, but not with alcohol."

10. James F. Light, *Nathanael West: An Interpretive Study* (Evanston: Northwestern University Press, 1961), p. 177.

11. Nathanael West, "Some Notes on Miss L.," *Contempo,* Vol. III, No. 9 (May 15, 1933), p. 2.

12. Elizabeth Drew, "Introduction to *The Waste Land*" in *Major British Writers,* ed. by G. B. Harrison (New York: Harcourt, Brace & World, Inc., 1959), p. 830.

13. This suggests that the following remark about Claude reveals something of West's own attitude toward his art: "He was a master of an involved comic rhetoric that permitted him to express his moral indignation and still keep his reputation for worldliness and wit." (p. 17)

14. Eliot, in line 60 of *The Waste Land,* refers to London as an "Unreal City," but the compressed allusions to Dante, Webster, and Baudelaire cause the city of London to take on universal proportions.

15. Eliot has the following note attached to line 60: "Cf. Baudelaire: 'Fourmillante cité, cité pleine de rêves,/ Où le spectre en plein jour raccroche le passant.'" The translation of this note is Miss Drew's, *op. cit.,* p. 832. Since the influence of Baudelaire is indisputable, it is impossible to know whether West had Baudelaire's poem or Eliot's note in mind. It is even possible that he had neither in mind. That West had no intention of creating a realistic atmosphere, however, is clearly borne out by his reference to "'the peculiar half-world which I attempted to create.'" See Light, p. 158.

16. See *The Waste Land,* lines 365ff.

17. In fact, only one is certain. There are numerous suggestions, though no direct evidence, that Faye sleeps with Earle as well as Mig.

18. Quoted by Light. See pp. 152-53.

19. Quoted by Light. See p. 152.

20. Chapters 1, 6, 7, 10, 18, 21, 25.

21. Hyman, p. 45.

22. Otto Fenichel, M.D., *The Psychoanalytic Theory of Neurosis* (New York: W. W. Norton and Co., Inc., 1945), p. 341.

23. Homer seems to be suffering from a "reactive type" character disorder. Fenichel notes: "They all betray themselves in one or more ways: by mere fatigue and a general inhibition due to economic impoverishment, by their cramped nature and rigidity, or by the warded-off impulses breaking through, either directly or in a distorted form, either in actions or in dreams. All reactive-type character traits, therefore, limit the flexibility of the person, for he is capable neither of full satisfaction nor of sublimation." (p. 471)

24. Fenichel notes that "impairment of the function of sleep is one of the most common neurotic manifestations and is encountered in almost every neurosis; . . . fear of sleep means fear of the unconscious wishes that may arise in sleep. . . . Fear of sleep then is a fear of dreaming, that is, of a failure of repression. . . . The fear of sleep or of falling asleep is very often a fear of the temptation to masturbate" (pp. 189-90). So successfully does Homer repress his desires that he literally sleeps the sleep of the dead.

25. *Ibid.,* p. 231.

26. Fenichel notes: "Acute worries . . . particularly sexual excitement make for sleeplessness." "The cathexis of the repressed [wishes] . . . either makes sleeping impossible or impairs its refreshing effect." (p. 189)

27. Fenichel notes: "In tics, a movement that was once the con-

comitant sign of an affect (sexual excitement, rage, anxiety, grief, triumph, embarrassment) has become an equivalent of this affect, and appears instead of the warded-off affect." "These connections are clearest in those cases that resemble in their structure hysterical spells. Genital masturbation, after repression, may be displaced from below and makes its appearance as a tic." (p. 318)

28. *Ibid.*, p. 213.

VIII. "WESTIAN MAN"

1. James F. Light, *Nathanael West: An Interpretive Study* (Evanston: Northwestern University Press, 1961), p. 24.

2. Nathanael West, "Some Notes on Miss L.," *Contempo*, Vol. III, No. 9 (May 15, 1933).

3. One is tempted to wonder whether West's images in *Balso Snell* (the bowels of the Trojan Horse) are not conscious symbols.

4. William Carlos Williams, "Sordid? Good God," *Contempo*, Vol. III, No. 11 (July 25, 1933), p. 8.

5. Light, p. 72.

IX. "HE CHARTS OUR WORLD"

1. Wallace Fowlie, *Age of Surrealism* (Bloomington: Indiana University Press, 1950), p. 26.

2. *Ibid.*, p. 18.

3. Nathan A. Scott, "Religious Symbolism in Contemporary Literature," in *Religious Symbolism*, ed. by F. Ernest Johnson (New York: The Institute for Religious and Social Studies, 1955), pp. 168-69. The four myths are the myth of moral isolation, of man as part of the mass of "homeless derelicts in search of self-definition and the Mystery of Being" (p. 170); the myth of the wasteland, of the distance of God; the myth of the quest; and the myth of beatitude.

4. *Ibid.*, p. 170. Scott, in his discussion of the city and the modern mythic characters who populate it, makes the following remark about Kafka—a remark so applicable to West that we need only substitute his name for Kafka's: "It is perhaps in the novels of Franz Kafka . . . that we get the most archetypal presentation of the contemporary hero. His is the religious consciousness of our age. . . . I mean that Kafka's is 'a mind which contains the terrors and nightmares of the age which most of us can't face.' What is perhaps first to be remarked upon is the atmosphere of isolation that pervades his books, enveloping

and conditioning the destiny of his hero. . . . At the center of his novels there is always the single individual, the lonely and uprooted 'isolato,' for whom there is no fixed abode and who, in becoming a kind of clown, grows 'more conscious of his center, of his distance from God, of the mechanical awkwardness of his gestures, of the dizzying somersaults his spirit performs before the revolving universe and the eternal peace of God.'" (pp. 170-71)

5. *Ibid.*, p. 176.

6. Harold Clurman, "Edward Albee in the American Theatre," program notes to *Who's Afraid of Virginia Woolf* by Edward Albee (Columbia Records), pp. 4-5.

7. Eliseo Vivas, *D. H. Lawrence: The Failure and the Triumph of Art* (Evanston: Northwestern University Press, 1960), pp. 271-72.

Index